Euphoric Recall

A true story of grit and hope

Aidan Martin

guts publishing

Published in London by Guts Publishing Ltd, 2020.

Cover art © 2020 Mark Deans
Cover design © 2020 Julianne Ingles

ISBN 978-1-9998823-6-5 (paperback)
978-1-9998823-7-2 (ebook)

Printed in the UK

www.gutspublishing.com

I dedicate this book to anyone who has suffered with addiction, trauma, suicide and mental health issues. I dedicate it to the working class. I dedicate it to the bittersweet streets of Ladywell. You will always be my first love. To all my pals 'fae Heatherbank'. To all the ones (so many) who helped me in life. And to anyone out there still struggling I dedicate it to you. Don't give up!

Author's Note

When this book was still a raw manuscript, I needed something to visualise. I needed a front cover. Just as I had finished writing the first draft I realised Mark was trying his hand at painting and drawing.

I'd always known his artistic side as a singer/songwriter. Acoustic songs that always sent me into deep crevices of sentimental thought. A safe little place in my mind for me to connect to a catalogue of moments lived. Whether those moments were joyous or torturous it was always an experience worth having.

I put the question to him about doing a sketch for me. Purely to help a mate out. Give me something to visualise before I started pitching this to publishers. Selfless as always, Mark was eager to help me. He wanted to read the manuscript so he could understand the tone. I knew in that moment that our life-long friendship was about to evolve once more. He was about to learn some brutal realities about my life. I put my trust in him. Something I have never regretted doing in all the years I've known him.

Much was discussed between us as he read the story. I will keep that between me and Mark to avoid spoilers. But he told me had a 'wee sketch' for me to look at. When he sent it over I was in shock. I was numb. I was amazed. *Now* my book felt real. *Now* I had the final piece of my story. Mark didn't just draw me a sketch. He drew my life. He drew my suffering. He drew my recovery. He drew my front cover. I knew from that moment that all my pitches to publishers would have a side story. That side story was 'two lads fae the scheme wae a big fucking dream'. Working together on the most intimate project of my life.

Folks, please let me introduce you to my friend *and* illustrator. The talented, unassuming and bighearted man that we call Mark Deans. And I should tell you that he is not just my illustrator. Going on this journey has been very exposing and at times traumatic to re-live. Mark has had my back throughout everything. I couldn't have done it without him.

For all my future work, Mark will be my illustrator. We will be like the 'schemey' Scottish version of Roald Dahl and Sir Quentin Blake. We dream of having our own studio. Which reminds me, keep your eyes peeled for our next collaboration currently in progress. A Scottish working-class mystery fiction called 'Where the fuck is Phil?' based on the trance culture of the early noughties.

Introduction

After the death of a family member, a furious urge came over me. An urge to write. I'd always known I had lived through enough trauma to last three lifetimes. People would say that throwaway phrase 'you should write a book.' But it was bigger than that. I had to face up to everything. And there was so much to tackle. I knew there was only one place to start. One brutal place I had to revisit in order to tell the rest of the story. Chapter One. Groomed.

For almost twenty years I've held onto the brutal past. Now it's time to let it all out. All of it. The whole story. Not just Chapter One. You see men like me feel too afraid to talk. Terrified. Addiction is constantly stereotyped, stigmatised and shamed. I am now on a journey to speak out and smash through all of that. I want to open the conversation up. Real fucking talk. So I've written down my pain. My recovery. My life.

These events are told from my point of view. Nothing has been exaggerated. When you read the extremes, you might be tempted to think they have been. That's what makes them extremes.

Some people have chosen to have their real names in this book. Others have pseudonyms. So if you grew up with me you might read a name and not know who it is. I have protected the identities of most. I want people to know that it is not my intention to hurt others by mentioning them in my story. But it would be impossible to leave out certain 'characters' from my life who had such an impact on me.

One example is drug dealers. I have not named or shamed anyone. And most of my dealers have been condensed into a handful of 'characters' in the book. But those involved in some of the brutal times will know it is them I am referring to. For example, when someone tries to take your life, you can't leave it out. Sorry about that. Hopefully if such a person *does* read this, we can meet up for a coffee and a chat. Maybe even hug it out.

One unavoidable relationship discussed is with my dad. It was a tough relationship and it is impossible not to discuss it. But once you have read the whole book you will see this isn't about blaming others and putting myself on a pedestal. The person I *really* point the finger at in this story is myself. This is about *my* life. My mistakes. My shame. My recovery.

Finally I feel like I can speak out. It is time to destroy stigma, stereotypes and shame.

This is just the beginning.

Aidan

Author Acknowledgements

There are far too many people I need to thank and acknowledge. It would take me another book to explain it all. So I will just list as many of them as possible below in no particular order —

Sam, Quinn and Katie—my world, my heartbeat, my oxygen, my everything. You have stood by me through everything. Mum—my guardian angel. Without you none of this would be happening. You are the best person I have ever known in my entire life. You always believed in me. You never give up. Dad—our relationship has been a tough one, but I will always be grateful for the fact you stepped into the 'father' role and done your best by me. Gran and Grandad—like second parents to me. Love you so much it makes my heart burst. DJ—I love you with all my heart wee man. Forever. Shayne—always my hero. Always my saviour. Always got my back. Always got yours too. Neil—I love you Cuz. You have the biggest heart in the world. My next book is based on you. Come on the ride with me man. Div—my oldest friend of them all. It has been a long arduous path at times my friend. Had some of our best and worst times in this lifetime together. You will always be my first ever friend. Your loyalty was like no other in those crazy days. My boys—Sneddon, Jamie, Miller, Alex and Sergie. I love you all. Colin—I'll never forget the years we had together my friend. Brother's for life. It made for some good fucking chapters. We could write a whole book about it. Maybe we will. Mark K—my straight-laced friend, ha! Always the good example in my life. When I was in the gutter

I watched you achieve great heights. It showed me it was possible. Your lack of mention in this book is purely because you avoided that lifestyle. But I love you dearly. To the person I call 'Cassie' in the book—thank you for your forgiveness and blessing. To the person I call 'Rachel' in the book—thank you for your forgiveness and blessing. Mark Deans—I love you Catface. Sharing this ride with you has been the ultimate journey. The journey continues. Weirdly you are not mentioned in this book. But you are certainly in the next one! Alan—meeting you changed my entire life. No such thing as coincidence. Cammy—just because I love you my German friend. Trees are no longer boring. Barrie Mulligan (Photography)—working with you on our book promo video was a privilege. I've made a friend for life. Looking forward to more collaborations. To the band Dictator—for letting us use your epic music (Taped Up) in our promo video. Hopefully we work together again. David Miller (who runs Goodfella's Barber Lounge in Easter Bankton, Murieston)—thank you. Forever grateful. When people read the book they will understand why. Fellowship—my recovery fellowship keeps me clean. Thank you to everyone in it who keeps me well. You are the foundation for my whole life. At my first ever meeting there was a person there on their own. Thank you to that person for being there that day. SD—you know who you are. We are on different paths for now it seems. But you had my back when I needed it most. I will always love you. Big Kev, Dave, Eddie, Julianne & Boydy—You all know why you are mentioned here. You all helped me back from relapses. The person I call 'Kirsty'—we had our ups and downs. But we love one thing the same. I will always love and respect you for that 'role' you play. Even when we do see things differently. Eoin—you know why your name is here. Thank you for everything. 'Dr Fred'—in my book I call you Dr Fred but we both know who you are. Thank you for everything. You have played a huge role in my life. Brian—thanks for pulling me out of drug dens all the way back then and telling me what an addict was. Stewart/Stubo—forever missed. I am still putting "one foot in front of the other" just like you taught me. Irene—forever missed. Thanks for the advice which I will never forget. It went like this: "Keep it real Aidan. None of that Uni shite." West Lothian Drug and Alcohol Service—thanks for putting me on the path to recovery. Darren—thanks for proofreading all of this when it was just an idea. I made you promise to tell me if it was shite. I trusted you and you had my back. Proud of our friendship. Proud of your achievements. You sir, are a warrior. My other Sam—one of my best friends. I love you dearly. You made student life a laugh, even when times were tough. Gemma—thank you for helping me to visualise and practice the laws of attraction. 'Pedro'—thank you is all I need to say here. I will find you once the book is released. West Lothian College: Lynda, Fiona, Maggie, Amanda & Ernie—thank you for educating me. Thank you for building me back up from nothing. Thank you for believing in me. Glasgow Caledonian University—thank you for educating me and giving me a chance. NHS—when you read the book you will understand. Thank you to our wonderful and invaluable NHS. Professionals—different professionals at different points have intervened and helped me get here today. Thank you. Russel Brand—it goes without saying, he is an inspiration to me and made me feel safer to speak out. Graham Macindoe & Susan Stellin—for the book 'Chancers' which inspired me to write my own. Thank you Graham for taking the time to read Chapter One when I was just at the beginning of all of this. Your encouragement gave me belief. Julianne Ingles & Guts Publishing—my publisher/editor and my teacher through this whole experience as a first-time author. You took a chance on me. I will be grateful for the rest of my life. Anyone I haven't mentioned—there are so many people I owe gratitude to and I can't list them all or recall them all. Ladywell—my first love. Always. I want to make you famous. All the characters. All the experiences. Brutal *and* beautiful. These experiences need to be told. Watch out for my next book. My *Higher Power*—whatever you are, wherever you are, thank you for saving me.

Illustrator Acknowledgements

I would like to say the biggest thank you to Aidan for allowing me to be a part of something so huge, so important to him and now to me. I'd like to pay gratitude to my mum and dad for always being open minded and encouraging in all my pursuits. To Robyn, for always pushing me in my arts. All the ladies and gentlemen of the PHS, we will ride again. Thank you guys for always holding me up. To Jo, without whom 2020 would have been even more unbearable. Lastly, thank you to Guts Publishing for believing in this journey.

Mark Deans

Euphoric Recall

Chapter One:
Groomed

I stood outside of that McDonald's with my heart racing. It was a dark winter evening and I could feel the cold air sharply stinging my cheeks. Lying to my Mum about who I was meeting didn't feel great. What was I supposed to do though? I could hardly tell her I was actually here to meet a man I had been talking to on the Internet instead of the 'friends' I was allegedly meeting. I was only fifteen. Still in school. As she drove off, I felt a horrible sense of having betrayed her. Writing this now I feel it was an even greater betrayal to my younger self. I was already on the way to ending my childhood innocence and yet I had no idea of the impact those moments would have on my entire life.

Ruminating now as an addict in recovery from substance abuse and sexual addiction, I have the gift of hindsight. Through recovery, education, therapy and life experience I can better analyse exactly *how* I became a schoolboy waiting for this older man to drive all the way up to Livingston, Scotland, from England to meet me. At the time, however, I had no clue. I still thought shouting out the words 'cheese and ham' as the teachers read out pupils' names from the class register was utterly hilarious, as did my group of friends. I was also suicidal and vulnerable, often thinking of ways to end my life or fantasising about being somewhere else, anywhere else, completely out of my own head.

Checking my pay-as-you-go mobile phone, which I had funded through my paper round, I knew *he* was on his way, almost near. My imagination ran wild wondering what he looked like and exactly what was going to happen once we met. We had never seen each other, never sent pictures or spoken on webcam. We had only chatted online or on the phone. Our conversations took place in chat rooms mostly. At that time all I knew was that he was supportive, and he understood me. He always sounded cheery on the phone and his Northern English accent made me trust him all the more. My mother, aunties and uncles all had Manchester or 'Manc' accents from growing up in Salford. So when Derek spoke in that Northern twang, I believed that he was warm and humorous too.

More than anything else, I was just happy to be in the world of fantasy, out of my reality as a struggling-to-cope, suicidal teenage boy. Already, at such a young age, my ever-growing addictions were taking hold of me and my mental health, but much like this rapidly approaching encounter with *him*, I had no grasp of the enormity of it. Nowhere near.

Pacing back and forward, teeth chattering, I kept my eyes peeled for a white van. That was all I had to go on. He told me he owned a textile company and that his work took him to West Lothian, where I lived. Livingston, West Lothian. Oddly enough, I recall this being one of the first conversations we ever had. Where we both lived. As an immature young boy, I had no reason to think any more of it or to question it.

2

With every passing van my heart smashed against my chest a little harder. Thoughts invaded my consciousness in frenetic fashion. Nerves truly had me now. What would he look like? I knew what I looked like. Skinny, blonde hair, blue eyes, freckles and tall with slightly protruding teeth that I hadn't quite grown into. I wore black nylon tracksuit bottoms, trainers and a sports hoody, much like many other gangly teenage boys of my generation in the early 'noughties'.

I wouldn't have to wonder what he looked like for much longer. An ordinary looking white work van pulled slowly into the McDonald's' car park. Headlights blinded my eyes as the warmth of my accelerated breathing mixed with the ice-cold air. Once the lights dimmed, I got a glimpse of the man at the steering wheel peering back at me, and it took me by surprise.

Derek waved me over to the van, and now that this was a reality my adolescent mind raced and my body began to pulsate with a blend of adrenaline, fear and nerves. He looked old and chubby, like someone's grandad. Those were the thoughts in my mind. I began to question everything. "What am I doing here? Should I run away? *Can* I run away? I'm not gay so *why* am I here meeting this older man?" I kept thinking, "He's driven all this way so surely I *have* to meet him?" No longer was I in the safety of fantasy, sitting behind a computer screen in my dad's study with a keyboard or in my bedroom on my brick-like mobile phone, where at any moment I could press the red 'end call' button and escape. Here I was, very much in a real situation, frozen on the spot and faced with danger. Then without thought, like an out-of-body experience as if watching myself from afar, I walked towards his van.

3

Falsely and naively I told myself that simply getting in the van wouldn't mean anything and I could get out of this whenever I wanted. This warped thinking would contribute to many years of compulsive behaviour in my life still to come as I would be gripped in the brutal world of substance and sexual addiction. As for right there in that moment, this ruling thought of 'act now, think later' took me into Derek's van where I got a better look at the man I had been speaking to since I was fourteen, almost a year leading up to this furtive meeting.

"Hi Aidan!" he said in a booming Northern accent as I sat down in the passenger seat, acutely aware that he centrally locked the doors. Waves of claustrophobia and panic engulfed me. "What happens now?" I thought. For the first time in my life that Northern accent, usually a nostalgic expression of love, humour and safety, was causing distress and alarm. And just like that, we drove off. My senses were in overdrive. The sound of the handbrake creaking, peddles being pressed and the ticking of the indicators roared in my brain. It didn't just feel like we were driving away from McDonald's. I felt like I was being driven away from safety. I was in a world of the unknown now. A terrifying place to be.

Derek didn't look or behave like someone to be terrified of in any particular way. His glasses magnified his eyes. I was aware of his rogue eyebrow hairs sticking out in places. He smelled of coffee and had slightly olive skin tinged by age. His hands were small but thick. He had dark hair, greying in places, with a tanned bald spot at the back. I noticed he wore a hi-vis vest over his white shirt, which his stomach swelled from. He had black trousers on. What creeped me out instantly

4

was his smile. It was crooked. As though half of his face didn't want to conform.

Despite this no longer being fantasy, it wasn't reality for me either. I didn't feel like I was actually there. It was as though I was in a hypnotic trance, which may sound cliché, but it is the only way I can relay this truthfully. As we drove off, Derek spoke to me about how long the drive was and how busy he was with work. Everything felt so strange. So unreal. So numb. Seeing that I wasn't saying very much, I remember Derek pointing out how shy I was compared to how outgoing I had been in conversation online. It was true. We had spoken of all sorts online.

Regularly I had told Derek how suicidal I was. He would listen. I would tell him how I was struggling at school and how hard my dad was on me. Derek would take my side. Being a young lad who never knew his biological father and struggled with a strict stepfather (who I call my dad), it felt amazing to have someone who understood me. One night, as I sat in my dad's study talking to Derek online, I was at breaking point. Crying hysterically, I told him I wanted to end my life. With tears splashing down onto the keyboard, I confided in Derek that I was crying. He told me he was crying too. It made me feel like we were connected.

I shared some of my other serious problems with Derek too. Like the day my dad stormed into my bedroom and threw down a £500 phone bill in disgust. He was furious with me. In shock, I hadn't realised I had run up such a massive bill. Oblivious at this stage in my life, my sexual addiction was already destroying my mind and soul. I had stolen porn magazines from our local shop in which I worked as a paper

5

boy. It was easy to steal porn magazines and VHS pornography tapes as I gathered the papers needed for my round each morning before school. In these magazines were phone numbers. Unbeknown to me they were premium rate.

One day I phoned one of the numbers, which had been described as phoning a dominatrix. I was drawn to phoning this number to experience degradation. I felt like a drunk sitting on the pub steps before opening time. I couldn't resist. Still far too young to understand why I sought out such self-harming treatment, that first phone call led to many, many more. Phoning those numbers gave me a rush I can only compare to a heroin addict's first hit. Complete ecstasy, escapism and carnal pleasure in one easy phone call. I didn't even need to do or say anything, it was all automated, like listening to a story. Easy for a teenager to get away with without any age verification needed.

Looking back now, the content of those automated messages was cheesy compared to the hardcore porn I had been accustomed to since I was ten years old. "Get down on your knees you snivelling little worm... lick my boots clean" or "I am wearing shiny, black, leather thigh-high boots with nine-inch heels for you to suck! ...get down and worship them" and the likes, always in an older woman's English accent.

Lacking self-awareness, I was experiencing the escalation of the disease of addiction. Without realising it, another habit or 'ritual' had begun. Every chance I got I was phoning, sneaking into my dad's study to pick up the phone and call the number. Once I had listened to a story once or twice it lacked the same impact and didn't do anything for me anymore, so I explored the plethora of numbers offered from the range of magazines I had been stealing and collecting.

Such calls now would arouse nothing more in me than laughter at how tame and ridiculous it sounds, however, I was desperate for interaction. The phone lines had been a buzz, but once I discovered chat rooms it was a game changer. It felt like an upgrade. I still got a good hit from the phone calls, but I couldn't go back to just listening to automated messages. I had become addicted to talking to real people. Or what I believed were real people. And anyway, I was about to be caught out for my secret phone calls.

When Dad found out, it was one of my first experiences of the consequences of addiction. My automated phone calling habit came to a halt the day British Telecom sent my dad the bill and he phoned the numbers himself. That was a type of shame and degradation I certainly didn't enjoy. Cringe and embarrassment too, especially when my very straight-laced, Catholic dad brought me to task. Feeling exposed like that wounded me with feelings of guilt that I didn't know how to handle.

Luckily, Derek was there. He placated me as I ranted about how hard my dad was on me. Pandering to my young desires, I distinctly remember Derek supporting and justifying my behaviour. Yet again, he understood me. Perhaps this opened the door to discussing sexual fantasies with each other. I can't quite recall the first time that happened. But it did.

During conversation I even indignantly expressed to Derek my anger at my dad telling me I would be paying the bill every week from my £15-per-week paper round earnings and my £10-a-week pocket money. This was a hammer blow at a time when I had recently discovered the joy of straight vodka and whiskey, purchased from a schoolmate each week who stole it out of his father's small, family-run shop. Part of the reason I told Derek this was to hint for some money to help me pay my dad. Derek was unable to help me pay it, he claimed, but he did want to buy me a new watch.

Fast forward to the moment in hand and here we were, in his van, talking in person. Or should I say Derek was talking and I was listening. Almost laughing, he said words to me I will never forget for as long as I live. He repeated these particular words a few times: "You look like a scared rabbit in the headlights," as though we were on our way to a theme park to ride a scary rollercoaster for the first time. In truth we were on our way somewhere far scarier. We were driving to a local hotel where I would present as Derek's nephew, carefully coached as to what I should say in the unlikely event of anyone questioning why our accents didn't match up. He had even gone to the effort of specifically asking for two separate beds to make this clandestine meeting seem all the more innocent.

Standing in front of the receptionist I was on high alert and the things capturing my attention seem strange to me even now. For example, I was extremely aware of how squishy the carpet felt under my feet or how there were framed pictures on walls looking lost against a backdrop of long white corridors. It was a woman on reception, yet I cannot recall her face or any of her features. What I do remember, is that Derek had to write both of our names down. He gave me his surname. That was the most surreal thing of all, to see my first name followed by this stranger's surname, my online friend who felt different to me now that I was standing next to him pretending to be his nephew.

Nonchalantly, Derek chatted away to the receptionist about how he was up in Scotland seeing family and working. Clearly at ease with this process of lying, it felt like a pre-emptive strike. Truth be told I wanted them to talk for hours. I needed time. I wanted to run away but it felt far too late for that. Regrettably, just like my porn habit, things continued escalating and once all the formalities were completed the receptionist handed Derek a key with a cheap looking plastic fob with a door number. We wouldn't have to walk far. The room was on the same floor we were on.

Leading the way, Derek swung the keys around in his thick hands and was even whistling. Acting so normal yet with such incongruity felt like such a paradox. Hearing the key fob open the door sent shockwaves right through me. Fear gripped me. With each step, I walked closer to the end of my childhood. Trembling, I timorously followed Derek into the room. He closed the door behind him and repeated those awful words, forever etched in my brain: "What's the matter Aidan? You look like a scared rabbit in the headlights. I'm not gonna hurt you." I was already hurting. I was scared. I wanted to go home and get a hot cup of tea and watch movies in my bed, in the safety of my home, my parents in their room and my wee brother across the hall in his room.

Telling me to sit down, Derek began to remove his outer clothing, hi-vis vest, boots, belt and so on. I sat down on the edge of the double bed, noticing a single bed made up near the window. I was, of course, there as his nephew, so that single bed was supposed to be mine. Yet again I became aware of

9

silly things. The small kettle and cups with little biscuits on offer beside the tea and coffee. A small remote control on the bedside table for the television. I could see glimpses of the car park through the curtains that Derek went over to close.

Derek turned to look at me. He stared for a long time. It felt like a lifetime to me. He was sweating and breathing heavily. From the look on his face and the prolonged silence it seemed like he was disappointed at how shy I was. He set up a laptop as he spoke to me, repeating how scared I looked. As he stood up I noticed something I hadn't previously. He was short. Shorter than me. It feels funny to say but he reminded me of a gnome without the beard. This really hit me hard in that moment. I really didn't know anything about this man at all, did I? Online you build up an image of someone, the image they give you and your mind fills in the blanks with qualities you would like them to have. I had been searching for something in those chatrooms, or someone, and I *did* discuss sexual fantasies, but I was the child and I was vulnerable.

To put me at ease, Derek suggested I relax as he went for a shower. But not before he presented me with two gifts. One was in a box and I opened it to see a brand-new waterproof, digital sports watch. It was black and red. Derek seemed so chuffed to give it to me whilst I felt confused over exactly how to feel, but I made sure to thank him. Finally, before going for his shower he pulled from a plastic carrier bag a bottle of Buckfast. I found this to be truly astonishing. If that moment hadn't felt so serious, I would have found the idea completely hilarious that this older English man would have walked into a corner shop and purchased a bottle of Buckfast.

10

To me, only young Scottish lads and girls drank this to get smashed out in the streets on a Friday night having all lied to our parents about our whereabouts. It reminded me of some of the lads in school I had difficulties with. It reminded me of the violent streets I grew up and hung out in. It reminded me my biological father never wanted me. Buckfast epitomised my working-class upbringing at a time in my life of painful suicidal thoughts and rebellious teenage behaviour. Yet here I was, in my apparent fantasy world, sitting on the edge of a double bed with a bottle of it in my hand as Derek went for a shower.

Twisting the top of the bottle, I swiftly removed the lid and knocked my head back to gulp down that cough syrup-like sweetness of this tonic wine. That familiar rush followed as it raced around my body. I genuinely loved that feeling every time I guzzled down Buckfast. It felt like leaving my consciousness behind and becoming someone else. This time was different though. I clung to the edge of that bed as though I was hanging from a dangerous cliff. Making my way through the bottle, I listened to the water ebbing away then the sound of a shower curtain swishing back.

Anxiously I waited, rooted to the spot on that double bed. Derek walked into the room and stood before me with water still running down his body and a white towel wrapped around his waist, failing to disguise how excited he was. It's curious the things you remember about an abuser. That bald patch on his head, the wry smile and swollen belly. His horrible overgrown toenails with a mole on one of his big toes. The fading arm tattoos. Which of all his characteristics, broke my heart the most. They reminded me of my grandad, who also

11

had fading arm tattoos. My grandad made me feel so loved and having his tattooed arms around me were always a feeling of protection, love, safety and acceptance. To see this man in front of me with tattoos much the same, damaged me in ways that would take years to understand.

Before anything happened, Derek pulled out one more surprise. A porn mag, his mobile phone and some premium rate numbers. Drunk as I was becoming, and grateful for the gift of the watch, I felt like I owed it to my friend to not let him down. I lay back on the double bed with my head resting on enormous soft pillows. Derek dialled a number on his phone and gave it to me. I placed the phone to my ear and listened to the familiar automated voice as I kept swigging the Buckfast to get the familiar rush of alcohol. Amongst all those familiar pleasures, what Derek did to me next was the most unfamiliar, horrific experience for a teenage boy who liked girls and was still a virgin.

I closed my eyes as Derek undressed me and performed a sex act on me. Never in my life had anyone touched me in such a way before. I wasn't homophobic, far from it. I just wasn't gay and if this had been with an adult woman, I wouldn't have been ready either. Not mentally or emotionally, if even physically. What Derek was doing to me felt alien and it felt wrong. I knew in my gut it was all wrong. I just lay there and hoped it would be over quick.

Something else was happening that I had never experienced before either. Suddenly the automated phone lines weren't working for me. To be blunt, I couldn't get an erection or get aroused. This frustrated Derek. I have to clarify that he was never hostile, ever. It always felt like I was letting down a friend and so I tried my best to keep going with it. Even the alcohol wasn't making me feel as invincible as it usually did. Finally giving up on that particular sex act, Derek changed positions and lay on top of me.

All I remember from this was his weight on top of me, looking up at him and seeing his face. It was expressionless. I was mentally gone from this moment onwards. I just wasn't there anymore. The automated phone voice now sounded like a continuous drone and I didn't move a muscle. I just waited for it to be over. Numb. Detached. Anesthetized from alcohol and shock. Eventually it was over and he rolled off me. Handing me his wet, white towel to clean myself up, he returned to the bathroom to do the same.

Then he came back with a big smile on his face that reminded me of the cheery man from the phone calls we used to have. Like a shapeshifter he got himself dressed, as I did too, and approached me with a big, warm hug. It felt like overcoming some kind of massive experience, as if I had survived a serious operation at hospital or something.

Before he dropped me back to that McDonald's and back to my life, forever changed, he sat next to me on the bed and just spoke. He told me his son had died some years before and how much it broke his heart. He spoke about his wife and his other children. He even, for some reason, told me he had a side job performing pop-up discos at weddings and that at certain times of the year he made an adequate wage from it. Like I mentioned before, it is a curious thing, the particulars you remember.

How do you go back to your so-called normal life after this? Feeling worthless inside is what had already sent me down this path of self-destruction. After meeting Derek, my sense of relationships and intimacy was corrupted and my identity over my sexuality confused.

Little could I have known, there was still worse to come in my life. I do not pinpoint this moment as defining my addictions. I was already on my way to becoming a full blown sexual and substances dual-addict. But it certainly sped up the process and provided me with trauma that would take years to understand and overcome. I still had many horrendous battles ahead. What I could never have imagined at that point in life, was that there would also be experiences beyond my wildest dreams in my future. Most importantly, I would go on a journey in which a *Higher Power* would guide my life in ways beyond human understanding, including the discovery of Derek's true identity.

Chapter Two:
Birth of an Addiction

Long before we had a home computer or the Internet, I discovered hardcore porn. My very first addiction began at the remarkably young age of ten. It continued developing through the stages of my life when I was leaving primary school and beginning high school. Contrary to some addiction stereotypes, parts of my childhood were very happy, however, there were many things I struggled with in my early teens that fuelled my desire for instant gratification. Once experienced, this became a life-long ambition second to none.

Born in 1986 to a working-class family, I grew up in an area called Ladywell. Much like the surrounding areas, it was made up of social housing schemes where people didn't have a lot. Some of the kids came from impoverished families that were on welfare or lacked credible role models. Livingston, only two decades old, was in continuous development to manage the overspill from Glasgow and Edinburgh. Everyone in my street knew each other's names. The schooling system was extremely poor at my local high school with many troubled children from different areas—many of them socially deprived—all sandwiched in together. Fighting to survive was normal for lads like me.

When it came to matters such as attendance, behaviour and educational standards, my school had a very poor reputation. Bullying was so extreme that one of my classmates ended up being interviewed on the national TV show *GMTV* to discuss how suicidal she felt. The reason the poor girl was bullied? She had big breasts for her age. I recall seeing scores of people regularly chasing her home after school. Looking back, the frightening thing was that it didn't seem out of place to witness such events at the time.

I lived with my mum and my older brother Shayne, who many would confuse as my twin as we got older. By the time I was a few months old, my biological father was no longer in my life. He had a notorious reputation. Saughton Prison was a regular stopover for him. He was well known for wild partying, violent fights, womanising, and spending his earnings from oil rigs on substances. Working the rigs made him very well built and he often smashed up our home in drunken rages. My older brother still remembers it well. My grandparents, from Mum's side, lived around the corner and became second parents to my older brother and me. So much so that my brother ended up moving in with them in his early teens.

Working three jobs to provide for her family, my mum, like many other single parents of the time, relied on my grandparents for support. My biological father, who I refer to as Billy, was not involved. Mum and Billy were only in their early twenties. One of my mother's jobs was working as a barwoman. This is where she met the man who brought me up, technically my stepfather, but the man I grew to call Dad. His family emigrated from Ireland whilst Mum's family moved from Scotland to Manchester back to Scotland again. My mum's mother, my granny, was Irish too, so they shared that in common.

Growing up in Livingston—a town that was still developing—reflected my own struggles with my identity. Not knowing my biological father, throughout my childhood people would stop me in the street and say things like, "You're Billy's lad aren't you? ...You're his double!" before going off on a tangent about how outrageous he was. The stories were always told with such affection and nostalgia as if he were some kind of loveable rogue. Honestly, I always thought one day he would turn up wearing a leather jacket with some wild story about an adventure, explaining his absence from my life. That never happened though.

Violence, gang fights, drink and drug use were normal for lads in my street. It was a social norm to hear of people being stabbed, murdered, raped or houses being broken into. We even had a well-known, much-loved alcoholic in the area called 'Mad Rab' who all the kids would go and get a chase from. He hung around with other alcoholics outside the pub my parents worked in. Community was an important thing back then though. There was no social media like we have now. People spoke to each other in the street. Whenever you heard the ice cream van or the chippy van, the neighbours in the street would line up having conversations whilst puffing fags, some in their dressing gowns and slippers, ready to purchase their goods.

My favourite memories were playing football with my friends on this little patch of grass in the middle of our street. We played day and night. The hours came and went. We

17

would steal parts of fences from neighbours' gardens and use them to build football goals or gang huts in the woods. I even developed a fascination with ants and spent hours with my friends looking for hives under rocks or in rotten tree stumps, observing their little colonies at work. We made up loads of other games such as 'fugitive' in which one kid would be on the run whilst the rest of the street hunted down the outlaw! Imagination was key. Looking back I can see how much I thrived on fantasy.

I always had one eye on the older kids though. Everyone looked up to them with equal admiration and intimidation. They hung around in large groups wearing an assortment of clothes. This ranged from tracksuit bottoms and hooded tops to jeans with Rockport boots. Sometimes they sported thick gold chains hanging over their tee shirts which went well with the black eyes and 'nookies' on their necks. My friends and I often watched them getting smashed on White Lightning and MD2020. Seeing drug deals was just another norm. As were the times we saw them being chased by the police. When those kids were tearing up the streets I felt such a buzz and I wished it was me too. In contrast, I also remember these were the first times I would experience anxiety and fear in the pit of my stomach.

Fighting with other kids started to become another social norm for me. By the time I was ten I was sneaking hammers out of my parents' shed to protect myself against whichever group of lads I was fighting with. I almost got suspended from primary school for that. It was pure survival where I grew up. Much like my mother, I was gobby and never knew when to back down, especially if my friends were in trouble. There

18

were rarely any fair fights or 'square go's'. We fought in groups or if it was one-on-one people would jump in or weapons would be used. It was a no-win situation. If you lost the fight your pride and reputation was shattered. If you won the fight you had to watch your back for someone getting revenge on you and jumping you with their mates.

These experiences highlighted the difference between my relationship with my mum and dad as well. For example, when telling my mum that some lad was giving me grief she would tell me to close my fist and hit them right back. If I needed a cry, she would hug me and tell me she loved me. Her crazy sense of humour reflected that of my grandparents, and I felt accepted. My dad was a provider and showed his love in practical ways such as teaching us not to lie, and to work hard at school. He advocated taking care of your responsibilities in life. However, our relationship lacked affection and often felt stiff or cold. If I told my dad a kid at school was bullying me his response would be to tell a teacher. If I hit another kid back in self-defence, I got punished. I couldn't relate to that. I felt it wasn't a realistic expectation in the hostile environment I grew up in.

At the same time, everyone was constantly telling me how funny and wild my biological father Billy was. I don't mean this to come across too harshly, but I felt my dad never showed much interest in my life and passions. We didn't tell each other "I love you" very often. On one hand I felt like I couldn't live up to this myth-like legend of my biological father who quite frankly fucked off and abandoned us. On the other, I never felt a natural chemistry or acceptance with my dad. We were very different people.

Over the years other behaviours contributed to feeling alienated from my dad. Fantasy played a big role in how I functioned as a child. One of my rituals was to run around with a toy figure in my hand, in a world of my mind's creation. I particularly loved to do this with my collection of wrestling figures or my Teenage Mutant Ninja Turtles figures. At some stage my dad decided I was too old to do this. This meant I had to do it in secret. When caught doing it my dad would punish me, and it made me feel like I was a freak. Catching me in the act on one occasion, he threw my favourite wrestling figure, Virgil, in the bin. I felt devastated and misunderstood.

When my older brother Shayne moved into my grandparents' house, this created more problems for me. The more time I spent there, the more my dad tried to restrict me. He felt my grandparents had become too involved after my brother moved in, which wasn't an unreasonable assumption. What he could never understand was how accepted and normal I felt at my gran and grandad's house. All my dad had achieved by restricting me was adding more secrets to my life.

Cementing my feelings of disaffection for my dad were his authoritarian measures. I believe much of it came from his Catholic upbringing. I always felt *that* religion focused too heavily on shame and guilt. The birth of my younger brother Declan, when I was seven, magnified things. I witnessed my dad expressing a very real love, pride and affection for his infant son in ways I never felt from him. I certainly don't believe my dad meant to make me feel that way. But I felt that difference between me and my younger brother. Scunnering me with feelings of jealousy and envy, it only heightened my desire to be closer to my older brother and grandparents.

Whenever my dad stood in my way, I resented him. I have to clarify that my dad wasn't a bad man. He was never violent. He worked hard, and instilled good morals and values. He encouraged us to study hard at school and never lie. He taught us to work for a living and to pay our bills and be responsible. We had amazing birthdays, Christmases and family holidays. When he met my mother, she had two children and he took that responsibility on. I can only commend him for that. Growing up in an area where many kids had no boundaries or discipline, my dad made sure we had an abundance of both. Too much for my liking though.

Compensating for not being handy with his fists, instead my dad would punish me by making me stay in my bedroom with no toys for lengthy periods. Again, I must reiterate, he came from an old school background and was trying to guide and discipline us. But I hated it. Turning the safe haven of my bedroom into a little prison, where I could only look out the window to see my friends playing, felt like a punishment that didn't fit the crime. I just didn't feel loved by him unconditionally. I always felt like I had two fathers who didn't really love or want me. Double rejection.

The only male I felt close with was my grandad. I loved my grandparents so much. They were like Jack and Vera from *Coronation Street*. Granny worked in a local biscuit factory and Grandad worked the taxis. He had his own history, once serving a prison sentence for cheque fraud. Always a joker, he made me feel accepted, loved and genuinely cared for. I will forever treasure our trips to Ingliston market where my grandad, wearing his signature 'bunnet' cap, fulfilled his desire for unnecessary gadgets, much to my granny's displeasure. Granny had her own history too with spells in hospitals due to severe mental health issues. However, just like my grandad she made me feel loved, accepted and normal. This all being said, it would be a cruel twist of fate that my first addiction, leading me down a path that eventually led to Derek, began in their home.

It all began as a big joke actually. It was no secret that Grandad liked a bit of porn in his twilight years. We all had a good giggle when my mum bought him a one-year subscription to Television X on cable TV and he told her it was 'too soft'. My eldest cousin Neil still makes us all laugh when he tells the story of how Grandad would point at him on his way out the door and joke around saying, "Now dinnae you be looking for my special tapes son." Grandad was a big joker and when he wasn't behind the camera recording home videos, or giving us all a 'fiver for your pocket' from his money bag, he was cracking us up with his antics. Undeniably though, those 'special tapes' would be life changing for me once I found them.

Oval in shape, the wicker basket containing those VHS tapes was hidden away in the cupboard at the back of the living room. The story goes that all the taxi drivers would meet up regularly and swap tapes, no different from people sending each other porn clips on WhatsApp in today's culture. There were always six tapes in the basket and quite often they were brand new. Merely years away from the Internet boom, VHS tapes were still the best way to view hardcore porn. Once I discovered that first film I slipped it into the video recorder in anticipation. As I soaked in the seedy content, addiction took hold of me like a parasite on steroids.

What I saw next stunned me and by no means is this an attempt to sound like *Fifty Shades of Grey* or something. Keeping in mind I was ten years old with no prior exposure to porn, seeing six men standing over a gorgeous, white, blonde woman in what appeared to be an outdoor porch with mountains and sunshine in the background, masturbating and ejaculating all over her, was shocking to see. Shocking yet intriguing. Shocking yet clearly arousing to my previously untainted mind.

That wasn't all. They ejaculated all over her face. I would learn as I got older that this sexual act was known as a *Bukkake*. Bukkake, according to the Urban Dictionary when you Google it, simply means 'one sperm recipient, usually of the female variety, and at least 3 sperm donors. I have yet to find a description for the part that came next. Two sexy black women licked the sperm off the 'recipient's' face. Straight away I was hooked. Adrenaline was shooting through my ten-year-old body like a child on ecstasy. I couldn't wait to watch the other tapes and clung to them like precious diamonds.

Variety must have been a prerequisite for the taxi drivers as the movies contained all different kinds of extremes. I viewed what looked like a woman to me, with breasts and long hair, unveil a penis for other men to suck on. Whilst today's society will have more politically correct terminology, in the porn world opening up to me this was known as a *Shemale*. Not only was the porn extreme, at such a young age—and living in the 90s—I had no idea such things existed. It didn't end there.

23

Included in the selection were people peeing on each other or what is known as *Golden Showers*. There was another video that much like the Shemale video, confused my young mind. In it a white man began massaging and oiling up three black men. Abruptly the video took a turn when he started kissing their bums. At that age, I just saw a man kissing other men's bums. I am certain I don't need to advise on how things developed. I had never seen men do these things to each other. At that age I just knew some men loved each other like my mum and dad loved each other.

Graphic in nature, the videos included what one might call 'vanilla' porn too. Simply put, men and woman fucking each other. Not being intimate. Fucking. Hooked instantly, my very first destructive addiction was now born. Sleepovers at Gran and Grandad's house became even more important. In fact, they were a must. I even figured out how to access the Television X cable TV subscription. My grandad was right, compared to his videos it *was* soft. It didn't matter though as I would just watch cable in my brother's room whilst he was out with his mates until my grandad would go to bed to prepare for his early morning start on the taxis.

Grandad going to bed at night would prompt me to declare to him that I was going to watch wrestling in the living room to access 'the big TV'. Immediately upon the sound of his bedroom door shutting, I was in that cupboard raking through the oval wicker basket. I would watch tape after tape. Perched on my knees like a rapacious desperado in front of the TV screen, I viewed those images as if my life depended on it. Sleepovers at my gran and grandad's house became synonymous with getting my fix.

I was already clashing with my dad daily. It was one thing to lie about running around with toy figures or sneaking round to see my grandparents. Now though, I had an altogether new, insidious secret. Masturbation became a daily fix whether I had access to porn or not. My body still hadn't developed in a way where I would even ejaculate. But every time I did masturbate, it felt good. As Renton from *Trainspotting* would have said—whilst getting a hit—it felt "really fucking good".

I was becoming desensitized to sex, defiling my mind and soul and polluting any concept I had about intimate relationships. I was also developing unhealthy coping methods whilst becoming acclimatised to lying and deceiving as if it was second nature. Addiction was contaminating my everyday existence as I moved onto turbulent and difficult experiences at high school. This led to the beginning of those dangerous, suicidal teenage years.

Right around the corner lay my next depths of addiction. My parents moved us to a middle-class area to get me away from the violence I was getting caught up in. They weren't to know that alcohol, weed, speed and ecstasy were awaiting me with a devilish grin. A raging substance problem that would become destined to hold hands in matrimony with my porn habit. The disease of addiction was about to escalate further in my life as I began talking to Derek online, supercharged by the unexpected death of someone I loved dearly which shattered my heart into a million agonising pieces.

Chapter Three:
Pre-Warned but Never Prepared

Surviving high school amongst a roster of tumultuous children has to be considered one of my greatest achievements. It was four years of misery, appeased for brief periods by the antics of my ragtag friends and my secret coping methods. I learned more about how to avoid beatings and homework than I did about Maths or English. Protection from teachers was non-existent and aspirations were a foreign concept. Still, I always had porn to turn to, like a secret friend. Soon we would have the Internet and I would have Derek to turn to as well.

My participation in secondary school felt more like serving time in a young offender's institution. In fact, many of the pupils had futures in such abodes. It was during those early teen years that my behaviour and state of mind became a concern for my parents. Quoting Kurt Cobain lyrics at the breakfast table in front of my wee brother unsettled them. Though it must have seemed like teenage rebellion it was actually suicidal thoughts spilling out. It was like the darkness I felt inside connected with Nirvana songs. The fact that Cobain had committed suicide made them more appealing.

With my secret porn habit intact, problems were piling up at school. Picture the environment. My school contained many underprivileged children that Charles Murray might refer to as an *Underclass*. All squeezed in together from competing local areas, we were like rats in a cage fighting for scraps. Not nearly enough to go around. We may have only been young teenagers, but gang rivalry was rife in nature. Mob mentality was common. No one questioned it. Just like the competing rats, we turned on one another.

What ensued was a hotbed of hatred and heated desire to be noticed. The song 'I Wanna Be Adored' by The Stone Roses comes to mind. Street mentality flooded the classrooms and dinner halls, whilst fire exits were used to flee bullies instead of smoking flames. I spent four years at war with many different kids. My friends always had my back. One time they formed a human wall and took hits to stop me taking a beating. Pure loyalty. There were two lads in particular that would go on to pose a serious threat to my life.

Ronnie was a chubby menace with a black French crop, a hoop in his left ear and a permanent grimace. We fought all through school. He was an angry little fucker and like many other hard lads in my school was always at his toughest when surrounded by his pals. Then there was Tommo who was a future resident of Her Majesty's Prison, for culpable homicide. He was skinny like me and had been a quiet lad. That changed when he became a drug dealer. I would very nearly end up skewered like a kebab on the ends of blades owned by these two.

Luckily I had a few solid friendships. My best friend David—who we called Div—was one. His balls of steel and Viking-like loyalty complimented his insanely funny view of the world. Much like me, he survived those years by not giving a fuck. We had each other's back and would always

27

take a hit for one another. Just like me, his biological father was absent when he needed him most. Luckily, his mother was made of steel. A salt of the earth type of woman who would do anything for her kids. Just like my mum. Div and I practically lived in each other's houses as kids. Ugly duckling syndrome was his biggest challenge, only blossoming from specs and teeth to Ashton Kutcher looks in his early twenties. Our rise and ultimate downfall would be a mutual love for drugs.

Our school compensated for a low standard of education with some outlandish teachers. We even named them ourselves. Mr McNee with the wobbly knee, table tits, hash heid and crater face to name but a few. I will let the reader determine how those infamous names in our school came to be. There were *some* genuinely good teachers too. For those ones I feel bad as I believe they tried their best to teach children in an unteachable environment. My computing teacher, Mr Williams, was forever pushed to the limits by our class. On one occasion I accidently sprayed him with a fire extinguisher. I had meant to spray my pals. One week's suspension was my punishment.

We also had a history teacher who found ways to relate to the class. We had invented an invisible classmate called Bob. She gave Bob his own desk, jotter and workbooks. Bob even got a pen. We loved her for it. Unfortunately though, teachers like that were few and far between. I never felt safe in school.

Deciding there were no solutions, I was more than happy to become part of the problem. I was suspended often. Kids like me wore detentions and punishment exercises like medals of honour. I only ever felt a sense of belonging when I was getting punished. My parents were at their wits' end. Enough was enough. They tried to pull me away from the trouble by moving us out of Ladywell. I was furious to be leaving Ladywell behind. It was all I knew. Looking back I can see how fortunate I was to have strong family support networks. But I couldn't see it at the time.

Moving middle-class to an area called Eliburn, Mum and Dad exploited the opportunity provided for their generation using Maggie Thatcher's 'Right to Buy' scheme. Our previously council-owned home became a stepping stone to a better life. They also knew it was my best chance of avoiding a future life of crime. There is a phrase in the recovery scene known as 'the geographical'. Simply put, this means to take your unmanageability from one place to another. This is exactly what I did.

My wee brother Declan, or DJ as everyone called him, thrived in Eliburn. Despite feeling jealous that my dad treated us differently, I loved my wee brother immensely. He wasn't streetwise like Shayne and I. Ladywell was too rough for someone as shy and gentle as DJ. I remember how heartbroken he was when he found out Shayne and I had a different biological father. Reassuring him, we fiercely asserted that there was no such thing as being a half-brother. Watching him settle into Eliburn and make friends was a blessing. I felt relieved he wouldn't have to experience what I did in Ladywell.

Eliburn would become bittersweet. But for now I was still in my Ladywell high school. I had refused my parents' offer to change schools and attend the more middle-class school closer to Eliburn. Deluded as it was, and despite the violence, I clung

29

to the belief that I belonged in Ladywell with my friends. So I split my life between both areas. My identity felt fractured. I was almost fourteen when we upgraded to middle-class. The streets of Eliburn, as beautiful as they were, felt alien to a lad like me who came from a housing scheme. And our house felt huge. This was a change in lifestyle for us all. It was in our new home that we bought our first brand new home computer. We had the Internet for the first time in our lives.

My fantasy world of porn was about to get very real. Before long I was regularly triggered by the sound of that AOL dial-up tone as I waited impatiently to be connected. That scratchy, grimy, electronic sound stimulated my brainwaves; pain and darkness slipping away every second closer to connection. Thinking about it now still gives me a euphoric recall. Once I started getting a fix online, it became my very own pain killer for life.

Teen Chat was my favourite chat room. The set-up was straightforward. One main room where everyone could chat and all conversations were visible. Or you could private message someone. Those were entirely intimate conversations between you and them. At the right-hand side of the screen was a list of all the different handles and avatars with their age and gender. It wasn't like social media of modern times. There were no statuses, pictures or videos. Anonymity was imperative, and I was soon to discover why.

Chocolate Puma was my handle. My avatar was a little blonde-haired face to reflect my own looks. My age and gender read: 14, male. ASL was the direct way to start up conversations with people. ASL meaning *Age, Sex, Location*.

Despite most profiles having an age, it was disconcerting to discover many of the profiles were fake.

Decades before the phrase was coined, older men were practising the skills of catfishing. Every time I logged on an older man would message me. Some as old as their late seventies. Some offered to buy me train tickets to places like Plymouth to go and live with them. Others would approach me with fantasies such as locking me in a cage. One man even had a well-thought-out plan for how he would tell everyone in his village I was a long-lost family member. In his words, we would "get on like a house on fire." Posing as a fourteen-year-old girl, a man in his seventies finally revealed his identity to me and said, "I don't think I could tame a chocolate puma!"

Most of the time I never indulged these people in conversation, despite this new world of adult communication capturing my imagination. When I started chatting with 'Derek-LFM' it was very different. The conversations were a slow burn. They weren't sexual at first. It was like we were pals. I found myself opening up to him about my life. He seemed interested in me. He was interested in learning about the things I liked and listened as I expressed my feelings. Talking to Derek in chatrooms became regular. We had established a bond and I trusted him. He was my friend and confidant. Topics of conversation included my struggles at school and issues with my dad.

Over time we began discussing sexual fantasies. I can't even remember how that crept in. As an adult I have gone over it many times in my head. At times I get angry with myself for being so naïve. So stupid. I don't understand how I could have been so streetwise yet so foolish online. But then I remember

31

how young I was. How suicidal I was. But most of all, how very young.

Derek would tell me he thought I might be gay. He emphasised how much he cared for me. He would tell me how worried he was as I told him of my tortured soul. I remember thinking— *"Finally, I have someone I can tell how suicidal I am who won't judge me."* It was our secret. He wanted my phone number too, so he could text me. He worried about the trouble I was getting into with other lads. He didn't want me to get hurt. The thing that surprised us both was that his job took him directly to Livingston, the town I lived in. What an outstanding coincidence.

Life wasn't all pain though. As I said before, despite having a suffering soul, there was still happiness in my life. When we arrived in Eliburn, Dad convinced me it would be a good idea to start up a paper round. I spoke to my local shop and they agreed they would pay me to deliver newspapers if I could gather enough interest. Practical as ever, my dad felt it would teach me a valuable life lesson about getting up early every morning to earn myself a crust. Dad was great at teaching us life lessons about being independent, I must admit. He once had me paint our garden fence to earn myself a better mobile phone. He was right about the paper round too, although he wasn't to know I would find a way to manipulate it to feed my secret addiction.

Chaos and hilarity commenced as my mother and I went around the local streets trying to drum up interest. She recalls that after about ten people saying they weren't interested I began to take teenage strops. "This is bloody pointless Mum, no one is interested!" I raged. Mum took a fit of laughing at my self-pitying antics. Tripping over someone's doorstep set us both off further as we tried to keep our composure. We were still in hysterics as we knocked on another door. When the woman opened the door, my mum, in her Manchester-Scottish accent, decided to take control. Pointing to me she mistakenly said, "This is my husband and he's trying to start up a paper round." Well that was it. We were ending ourselves with laughter! So much so that when we knocked at another house the poor woman opened her door to two strangers falling about laughing. Somehow, by the end of the night we acquired around twenty new customers for my round, but God knows how.

My parents were making every effort to build a new life and pull me out of the violence, but it was no use. In Eliburn we were having barbeques with our neighbours and street parties with fireworks. But in my Ladywell school fights with other groups of lads were progressing. Yet again I got suspended. This time for bursting Ronnie's nose in a defiant act of self-defence. I finally cornered him without his friends and let him have it. It felt fucking great to be honest.

Upon return from suspension there were threats on my life. I had dropped down to the lowest classes in school, amongst some of my enemies. They were *barely* what you could consider a class. We didn't learn anything. More like shoving the problem kids into a box and forgetting about them. One time my science teacher blatantly looked the other way as Ronnie and his mates hurled staplers at me. "You're fuckin' dead after class!" This was real. I knew they meant it. My friends weren't in this class either. I was completely alone.

When that teacher looked the other way, my heart sank. I ought to have expected it. Drug deals in the toilets and fire alarms being set off regularly were the tame parts of my schooling experience. Classes with teachers stoned out of their box with kids throwing everything from chairs to notebooks out the windows was more realistic. Racing against the clock, I was thinking of ways to escape but to no avail. As soon as that bell rang, I was a like a boxer flat out on the mat. It was game over. I got no further than the hallway before I was jumped and severely beaten.

Kicks to the head and ribs rained down on me and I blacked out in a world of pain. I woke up feeling as if I was blind in one eye. Somehow the beating got interrupted and I was bouncing from wall to wall looking for an exit. I wanted to cry. There was a lump in my throat and my eyes stung. I didn't want to let anyone see me that way though. Showing weakness in *that* school was not an option.

I stumbled through large double doors into the dinner hall, desperate to see my friends, especially Div. No luck. I couldn't see anyone. I was taking a risk no matter what I chose to do. I knew going outside would mean risking a weapon being used. Or at the very least being ripped apart by a pack of wild dogs. I kept stumbling around until I found safety. Finding a lockable room in the music department, I hid in a small cupboard amongst symbols and tambourines. My face throbbed in excruciating pain. I could taste blood in my mouth.

I felt completely hopeless and powerless sitting in that cupboard. Every year of high school had been like this. It was only for so long that my group of pals could survive being the underdogs. We were misfits. Truth be told I just wasn't as violent as the lads I was always fighting. Some of them seemed at ease with taking things to the next level. But the idea of jumping on someone's head or stabbing them felt sickening to me. Survival was day to day.

After what felt like enough time, I bolted through a fire exit onto the school field leading directly to my grandparents' street. Athleticism wasn't my calling, but I sprinted across that field like a cross-country racer. Getting in the front door felt like reaching safety. Just as I looked in the mirror to see my right eye completely burst open—the whites of my eyes blood red—my grandad walked into the hall.

"For God's sake son, what's happened to you?!" he asked. Wrapping his arms around me he held me close. "Where are the bastards?" he cried. "Take me to them now," he demanded. I just broke down. My older brother Shayne was forever bailing me out of trouble like this. Some of it my fault, but much of it was me trying to fight against the odds. Grandad seemed overly emotional, even under these circumstances. He said he needed to talk to me.

We went into my brother's room for privacy. Standing before me he said, "Son I need to talk to you. I am dying son. I have less than six months left."

"Don't be so daft Grandad," I replied, shrugging it off as another wild tale. This time though, it didn't feel very funny.

Grandad always told tall tales, so I didn't believe him. His jokes have become legendary in our family. Neil, my eldest cousin, said Grandad had fooled him for years saying that he was a secret agent. Likewise, I remember Grandad pulling similar tricks on me. Driving into his 'army base'—

which I now know was his taxi office—Grandad would tell me to duck down under the back seats to stay safe in case we got ambushed. Grandad would reassure me, "Don't worry son I have my gun," as he pointed his index finger at me. You see, he had me believing he could screw the top of his finger off and turn it into a pistol. Joking around as always, there *were* elements of truth though. He had served in the navy and lost his best friend Noddy. Maybe this was how he dealt with his own pain, turning it into laughter and adventure for his grandkids?

Here we were though, having this conversation, and this time he wasn't fooling around. This was my first *Higher Power* moment. Grandad hadn't seen a doctor. He wasn't diagnosed with anything. When I ask my family, they swear he never had a conversation like this with anyone else. Maybe he was worried he wouldn't be around to protect me from people, or from myself? In my heart I know he was aware that Shayne and I looked up to him as our father figure. Especially Shayne. Somehow, he must have known he didn't have long left in this world.

Denial took over. I rejected this information as false. Amidst this news, and the violence I was getting caught up in, even porn wasn't enough anymore. Timing is everything they say. So that day in Drama when my classmate Hamed informed us that he was selling half bottles of whiskey and vodka at a tenner a pop, the timing was perfect. It was like a little alcoholic tuck shop behind the black curtains in Drama class. Performances were going on Stage Left with budding actors, whilst deals were being struck by budding alcoholics backstage.

Twisting off the red lid from the vodka bottle or the black lid from the whiskey bottle and inhaling the smell of pure spirits was enough to make me feel high on its own. The sheer power I felt flowing through my veins just possessing these bottles felt incredible. I was even more excited about this than going online or watching porn. Porn felt like child's play compared to this. All I could think about was Friday coming around and meeting my friends and getting stuck into these bottles of straight vodka and whiskey.

When Friday finally arrived, we stood around in a circle, huddled together in the dark. As well as the hardcore booze we had alcopops like Big Beastie and Blue WKD. I was so fucking ready for this. Bottle tops off, head tilted back, and straight vodka gulped down without hesitation. My eyes must have rolled back into my head with that heavy-duty rush! Vodka flooded through my body and my brain began brimming with ultimate pleasure. I felt ten-foot fucking tall. Invincible, resilient and with unbreakable fortitude. Life was changed forever. I had climbed my Everest and I felt brand new.

Blackout drunk, that darkness, that horrible fucking darkness that followed me everywhere was lifted. Alcohol was like my weapon against it. My medicine. All those thoughts of killing myself, wondering how you actually *make* a noose, were gone. Jealousy, envy, anxiety, rejection, all gone. Panic, pain, and fear. Fear. FEAR. All fucking gone. The gut-wrenching pain of knowing that my biological father didn't want me, gone. Feeling unloved by my dad, gone. The problems with the local lads, gone too. "Give me more booze man... Just give me some fuckin' more." Logic evades me when I recall these moments. I just remember wanting to escape and alcohol took me to another planet. The hole in my soul needed filling. To quote Renton from *Trainspotting* once more, "But it's never enough."

Spiralling lower and lower, I stopped caring about anything. Derek would text me (pretending to be a girl in case my friends saw my messages) to ask if I was OK. Fantasising became more vivid. One night I dreamt I lived in the world of the TV show *Saved by the Bell*. If you haven't seen the show, it is about a bunch of teenagers in a California high school. Unlike me, the characters' problems were resolved by the end of each episode. Unlike my school, the teachers cared, and their lives seemed so amazing on the sun-kissed beaches of California. I can see why R.E.M. allegedly wrote the song 'Shiny Happy People' as a tongue-in-cheek jibe at critics who claimed they sang about misery too often. The shiny happy people in *Saved by the Bell* were not a reflection of real life. Not my real life anyway. The dream felt so profound, so real, that waking up from it was devastating. So profound was the disillusionment that it set me on a path to start planning the end of my life.

I threw myself into conversations with Derek. My pals were always there for me, but I felt like he was the only one who could truly understand. Before long I would find myself at that McDonald's, waiting for him, thinking I was meeting a friend.

Converging with those experiences with Derek was the first great loss in my life. My grandad was rushed into hospital on a Friday and told his body was completely riddled with cancer. He passed away the following Tuesday. It was a crushing blow for us all and created a chain reaction of events. To this day I have still never seen my brother Shayne break down and cry the way he did when we found out. I could barely hold him up as he crumbled in my arms. My mother was devastated beyond words and my sweet, funny, lively granny deteriorated overnight. This led to her diagnosis of bipolar disorder and chronic depression. She became an instant recluse. Granny 'died' as well that night, her body just didn't know it yet. As for me, I was numb.

Seeing my grandad in his hospital bed, dead with yellow, cold, rubbery skin, shattered me. I had never lost anyone before and despite his warning, nothing could have prepared me for how this would feel. He was the only man who made me feel like it was OK to just be me. I remember him lying in a funeral parlour with the song 'Sign Your Name' by Terence Trent D'Arby playing on a small CD player. Hearing that song still gives me chills to this day and yet I find comfort in that pain whenever I listen to it.

The last time I recall feeling like a child was right before I met Derek and right before I lost my grandfather. After this, I didn't give a fuck anymore. I was ready to die. I was willing to go to those lengths of violence that had scared me before. I was ready for war. I left school with no qualifications and took a job at the shop in which I had been a paper boy. I moved in with Shayne, Neil and Div in what became more of a drug den than a bachelor's pad. I began experimenting with ecstasy and speed. Sneaking into nightclubs using my brother's passport ID was another step into 'adulthood'. Although I thought losing Grandad and seeing Granny lose her mind was the worst pain imaginable, I was wrong. Tragedy was about to devastate our family and take us to depths of hell that no human should ever experience.

Chapter Four:
Diagnosis of Despair

Grandad dying provided a false sense of justification for my new ventures into heavy substance abuse. I was confused about my sexuality after secretly meeting Derek. What confused me most was still having contact with him. Leaving school with nothing to show but war wounds, I took up a job as a sales assistant. I helped get Div a job there too. This tied in nicely with my cousin Neil's grand idea that we all move in with him. We moved to another housing scheme in an area called Deans, much like Ladywell. By now I was sixteen and wanted away from my dad controlling me. Div and Shayne saw potential for a party house, and I liked their thinking. The four of us drove to a beach called Silver Sands. Drinking booze and smoking joints on the sandy beach, we fervently discussed all the exciting possibilities. After Grandad's death, we all just wanted to be together and our joined-up thinking was of the 'fuck it' mentality.

Eliburn had been a beautiful place to live but I felt like a fish out of water there. It was full of spacious houses, expensive cars and quite frankly kind and considerate neighbours with inspiring careers. Despite that, I missed the edgy, authentic realness of the people I grew up with in my working-class streets.

Instead of private driveways and Marks & Spencer shopping bags, I craved seeing people drinking Lambrini on couches in their front gardens with fags dangling from their lips. In Ladywell you wouldn't think twice if someone threw their TV over a garden fence and smashed it on the pavement. It was normal to see domestics in the street. To see someone accusing their partner of "shagging that wee slag Kerry-Anne" from down the road. In Eliburn if someone scratched their surname into a fence, they thought they were hard. For all the flaws in my logic, with my rose-coloured glasses, I just didn't feel middle-class. I was conditioned to a certain way of life and I missed the characters. So, I jumped into my new life of drug-fuelled partying in Deans with my boys. It nearly fucking killed me right enough.

The extreme recklessness of my life was lost on me. I had no self-belief, self-esteem or confidence. I certainly had no big plans for the future. Forever young was the war cry and the four of us tore into the party scene. Neil and Shayne were lucky enough to experience the rave scene. Me and Div caught the tail end of it. Trance music was massive and taking uppers elevated your senses to the beat of the banging tunes. Euphoria. That's what it felt like. Not at first though. My first experiences with drugs were horrendous. Only the covert addict within could condone going back for more.

After a heavy shift of drinking and smoking weed—with daylight creeping in through the curtains—someone brought out a little 'speed bomb'. It was twisted up in a tiny piece of toilet roll. "Want to try one?" I was asked. "Fucking right I do," came my reply. Everyone on it was speaking at a hundred miles an hour. Their jaws were swinging, and they were completely loved up, like it was never going to end. I wanted some of that fucking bliss. There was even a guy wearing yellow Marigold gloves scrubbing dishes intently. He was in his element. Unbelievable! "Give me a shot of that, now!" There is a scene in Shane Meadow's cult classic film *Dead Man's Shoes* identical to this. It makes me laugh with identification every time I watch it.

After devouring that speed bomb, I morphed from being tired and groggy to supremely energetic, loved up, and wired in an instant. The buzz was razor sharp and I felt yet another form of invincibility. It was so good I took another one. A 'double-dunter' we call that. There was no way I would make it to work the next day. Neil called in a sicky for me pretending to be my dad. With that fake family emergency called in, I decided now was the best time to phone a girl I really fancied from school. I was tripping balls on speed and wanted to declare my love for her.

Dialling her number, I was so high I couldn't even see properly. "Leeann, it's Aidan! Aye it's me. It's Aidan, it's Aidan, it's Aidan. Listen. Leeann, listen. We need to talk. Like I know we don't say it enough, but we really need to talk more often. Know what I mean? We should go for a pizza or something, like, 'cause you know I've always really liked you eh? And like, I know we don't see each other much but there is something there eh?" I was speeding, literally, without taking a breath to let her say anything. "So fuckin', eh, like, you know I am high as fuck man, but I wouldn't say it if I didn't mean it, you know that anyway. I just really fucking like you man. We should spend more time together. This isn't the drugs talking honestly, I really mean this. I mean like I am high, no fuckin' denying that, but I truly mean it. I love ye."

Now clearly, I cannot accurately recall what was said word for word, but I know this is the route it went down. I remember pacing uncontrollably, experiencing what felt like electricity pulsing through me as I spraffed nonsense. With amphetamines, like speed, I had no control over what I said. No sooner had a thought entered my brain than it left my mouth. The cringe and sheer embarrassment to be realised in the coming days were the least of my concerns. What goes up must come down. My body had no tolerance for speed yet I had just double-dunted. I was about to crash in a dangerous way.

Comedowns didn't happen gradually on uppers. I went from feeling instantly high to crashing down as though I had fallen from a skyscraper. To feel so high and then experience extreme waves of depression caused a drug-induced psychosis. The suicidal tendencies came thundering back. My brain couldn't handle it. I went from feeling that life was limitless to feeling like the world was a black, hopeless pit of despair. This gives insight into why addicts take more and more to keep the high alive and stave off that terrifying darkness they know is on the way. This would become my experience with all uppers. Emotional despair wasn't the only enemy on this occasion though. I wasn't prepared physically for this double speed bomb.

The first feeling I recall was my body freezing over and stiffening up. My head began to pound as if my skull was shattering from the inside out. My jaw tightened up like a vice grip as my teeth locked together. Like claws, my fingers tightened up too and I could feel my heart going like a treadmill on full pelt. I could barely catch a breath. I felt dizzy, nauseous and lightheaded. Aching skin was accompanied by severe cramping and I began to panic. Terrified and confused, I ran out of the house. Merely minutes before I was partying as if I were having the time of my life. Running across roads crying, I stumbled into a field. Neil caught up with me. He brought me back home and I began to cry harder and vomit everywhere, before eventually passing out.

I woke up almost a day later. I found myself lying on the sponge floor mattress that Div and I shared. I was in the box bedroom we also shared. *We sure were living like champions.* People were coming and going for days visiting me in there, as if I were dying in a hospital ward. I literally could not move. Daylight hurt my eyes. I was throwing up in a basin next to me and my body ached all over. Consequences of addiction were already in motion as I was absent from my job too. My parents taught me better than that. They worked hard for everything they had. I felt so ashamed as I lay there, unable to move.

Flashbacks of the phone call to Leeann hit me hard. I wanted the ground to open up and swallow me in the pathetic heap where I lay. Scary to think that I almost died, and my biggest concern was how I would look in the eyes of others. "Leeann will think I'm a fanny," I agonised. I could hear everyone partying downstairs again. "They're all going to think I'm a pussy!" Hearing them all having fun as the music blared made me feel jealous. So scared I was missing out, and so desperate to get out of my own head again. The exact minute I felt well enough to stand up, I stumbled downstairs, peeked my head through the door to the sound of cheers and asked for another hit. As the lyrics from the 'I Monster' song go, 'The party never ends, the game begins again' and I was off and running once more.

Inevitably, our party house didn't last long. Not because we burned ourselves out, which I am certain we would have. Instead we got into a fight with our next-door neighbour. Ironically it became a battle of who was the worst neighbour from partying the most. If either of us had been smart enough, we would have all partied together in harmony. But instead of that we let male bravado and misplaced egos take over. I must admit, we were acting like a bunch of arseholes and trying to play the hard men. Only we bit off more than we could chew, by far.

The fight took place in the middle of the street with this older neighbour, who admittedly was a lot bigger and tougher than us. There were three of us (me, Div and Shayne) against just him. I had a go first. Every punch I threw bounced right off his head. He took me down with ease and rag dolled me around. He intimidated us all and if he hadn't been outnumbered I think he would have hospitalised any one of us. Still, regardless of our strength in numbers, it was us who retreated with regret at what we had started.

By this time Neil had already abandoned the sinking ship of our party house. This left me, Shayne and Div to decide what we should do. By midnight, our neighbour was in the street with another man standing next to a car with the boot open looking in through our window. We all freaked the fuck out. What had we done? Who exactly had we just pissed off? That 'act now, think later' mentality was fucking me up again.

We did a moonlight flit, fleeing with whatever possessions we had the minute the coast was clear. We never dared to look back. The party house was over as quick as it began. But for me the partying, or should I say the *using*, had only just begun.

Tail firmly between my legs, I moved back in with my parents and my wee brother DJ. Back to 'Happyville'. Where lampposts never got kicked in, windows weren't egged, and you didn't have to hide your bins on bonfire night. God I still missed Ladywell and all that madness. I just loved being around chaos, it matched how I felt inside. I was still suicidal, but why kill myself when I could use hard substances? Suicide was plan B. Until then self-medicating was just fine. Don't get me wrong, I had my fair share of scraps with Eliburn kids too, but it wasn't the same. One time, one of the hard lads from Eliburn had started some shit with a lad half his size. Only the wee guy came from Ladywell and so he turned up with a baseball bat looking for the Eliburn kid. That was the difference really. I grew up on stories of guys murdering each other on bridges and petrol bombing each other's houses in Ladywell. I know those stories were at the extreme end. Ladywell was a *lot more* than that to many people, including myself. But the older I got the more I was pulled into the underbelly. In my heart I belonged there.

Was it because I also grew up on stories of Billy, my biological father, tearing up Ladywell in his own heyday when Livingston was first created? Quite possibly. I still ached for my identity to be put back together. It felt like a jigsaw puzzle with most of the pieces still missing. But Billy wasn't around. My only links to Ladywell now were Div and Shayne. Both moved in with my granny, who was still deteriorating after Grandad's death.

Speed wasn't a drug I stuck with for long. Ecstasy was much better. I was sneaking into clubs now where ecstasy was much easier and cheaper to access. Getting ID'd by bouncers was nothing to worry about. After they finished searching you meticulously for drugs and frisked you in front of the security cameras, they would slip three eccies into your wallet. Then they waited by the puggy machine for you to palm them a tenner as inconspicuously as possible like nothing went down. Much like the alcohol in my school days, the eccies made me feel drunk with power. I used to put three eccies in the back pocket of my jeans and swirl them around in my hand as I felt confidence surge through me.

Eccies truly were the love drug. I would even have loved Ronnie and Tommo had I bumped into them whilst I was high on eccies. Conversations in nightclubs when on eccies always consisted of dialogue such as, "I fucking love you brother! You are my bro, man. We are best friends. No we are fucking *more* than best friends. We are brothers for life. No matter what happens, ever, we are brothers for life man. And this isn't the drugs talking man. I fucking mean it. I love you." And that was when you were talking to a guy who just leant you his lighter for a fag. Just met, brothers for life.

The same happened when pulling girls in clubs. Eccies made me hallucinate and blurt out random things uncontrollably. One time I met this pretty, redhead girl in the local nightspot. I'd literally just met her that night. After pulling her I got chatting to some other girl, kissing her under green laser lights in a cloud of artificial smoke pumped onto the dance floor. To make your evening all that more magical, I guess. I was apparently having the time of my life again, tuned to the moon. When the redhead from before spotted this betrayal, she promptly poured a pint of snakebite (cider and blackcurrant) over my head. Quickly trying to make amends I sat her down to speak to her. Eccies, as they so often did, made me blurt out the craziest shit. As this girl started to walk away from me, I shouted, "But I love you though!" Crazier still is that I really believed I meant it, right up until the moment I heard myself say it out loud.

One of my funniest memories on ecstasy was seeing Div gouch on the floor of my brother's house. He started to scramble around looking for something. When we asked what he was looking for he shouted out, "I'm looking for the fucking flower-pot van keys, help me find them." Immediately after saying the words, with his flying-saucer-eyes widening, he reacted to this eccy trip going, "Waaaaaaooooow man." Or another occasion when my very straight-laced friend was out with us and I was eccied out of my face and told him the Football Association of Wales had sacked their manager Mark Hughes and offered me the job. I sincerely meant it as I was saying it in the moment until I realised I was tripping. Many lads my age played a computer game called Football Manager (or Championship Manager) and I think this is where my 'trip' originated from. That was the thing about substances though. In the beginning I loved them, even with the bad experiences. At *that* point the good times outweighed the bad.

Drug use also played a role in my manipulation of women. I was getting into relationships with girls I didn't know how to care about or treat properly. I could barely treat myself with any respect. Telling girls I loved them whilst high on drugs, knowing fine well I didn't, was cruel on my part. The truth was I didn't have a clue about relationships. They were a means to an end. Frivolous fun with no real credence in the idea of a loving connection.

One of those girls was Cassie. She was one of my best friends but also an on-off girlfriend and a fuck buddy. We had met some years before. She was a curvy and extremely pretty girl from South Africa. Her parents were Scottish, so she had a mixed accent. We took each other's virginity back in the party house, just before we all bailed from it. At least what my idea of virginity was. What happened with Derek still hadn't fully resonated with me.

Cassie gave me unconditional love and I shamefully treated her like an afterthought. As an adult looking back, I understand that I wasn't stable or mature enough to be with her. But it doesn't make me feel any better about the way I led her on. She is one of the best people I have ever known and had a pure heart.

Derek was still texting me and online chats had moved away from Dad's study. By now I had my own PC in my bedroom, and we spoke on MSN Messenger. I was getting older but rather than trying to make sense of what had happened with him, I kept pushing it to the back of my mind. I had convinced myself I wanted our meeting that night to happen. In fact, I even met him a few more times after that. The truth is I never wanted to admit that in this book. That part fucked me up the most. *Why did I keep meeting him? Why did I stay in touch?* It would be many years until therapy would help me answer these questions and remove the blame from myself.

For years I convinced myself that since I kept speaking to him after I turned the legal age of consent (sixteen in the UK), I clearly wanted him in my life. No matter how much those experiences damaged me, I could not blame him at all. Even with the knowledge that we had spoken since I was fourteen and met when I was fifteen. In fact, I felt like I *owed* him something, like I had let him down for not meeting him more regularly. Most times I bailed or stood him up. I made excuses and he would stress his disappointment. Again it felt like I was betraying a friend. The watch he gave me was hidden away under my bed and I never wore it again. More pressing matters were on my mind though and it wasn't Derek, porn *or* drugs.

DJ, my wee brother, was getting a lot of viral infections. He was ill a lot of the time. More troubling than this, he was crying a lot and didn't know why. He was ten years old, the same age I was when I discovered porn and began getting deeper into violence. The idea of someone bullying my innocent little brother made me feel enraged and sickened all at once. Reassuring him that anything he told me stayed between us, I succinctly asked him if he was being bullied. I already had a plan in mind of what I was going to do to the little bastards. DJ cried out in confusion, telling me it wasn't bullies. Doctors couldn't figure it out. They asked my parents if he might be depressed. Depressed? He was only ten, came from a loving family and went to a good school. He had plenty of friends and lived in a thriving street. DJ had a healthy, safe lifestyle. My parents kept on with the viral infection medication, despite its ineffectiveness.

51

Soon after this my wee brother had a very strange experience. Eating his Rice Krispies for breakfast, my mum asked him why he hadn't wiped his face. Nonplussed, DJ asked her what she meant. He had cereal stuck to the left side of his face, yet he hadn't realised. It came to his realisation, and my mother's horror, that his face was completely numb on the left side. In a flurry of panic my parents rushed DJ back to hospital, this time as an emergency patient. By now I was seventeen and had just started a new job as a credit controller. The office I worked in was just a short walk from Cassie's house. Upon finishing a shift one evening, I received a phone call from my mother as I walked towards Cassie's place.

Fighting tears my mum told me to get home as soon as possible. I begged her to tell me there and then exactly what the news was. I couldn't possibly wait until I got home! Her crying and the tone in her voice already confirmed it was something terrible. Mum was usually a happy, optimistic person, so I knew this must have been serious.

She simply said, "It's cancer," before we both began to cry hysterically down the phone. Frantically I made my way to Cassie's house. I collapsed to my knees and she cradled me like a helpless newborn. I cried in her arms as she and her sister tried to comfort me. "I don't want him to die," I wailed painfully, my heart ripping in two. "He won't die, please don't cry!" Cassie said, attempting to hold back her own tears. DJ was diagnosed with *Rhabdomyosarcoma*, one of the rarest soft tissue cancers in the world. It was sitting behind his left eye and tragically it was inoperable. The size of a lemon, it was just too close to his brain to operate. Our lives were about to be changed forever.

Chapter Five:
Dancing with Death

Sexual addiction was still a major problem for me. However, when we received the news of DJ's illness, my substance abuse escalated. I numbed the pain with ecstasy. My younger brother was dying. The best doctors the NHS could provide told us it was just a matter of time. Horrendous chemotherapy and radiotherapy treatments were the only options. All they could do was buy time. People deal with devastating news like this in different ways. My dad was a practical man. He took this crushing blow as factual. My mum had a 'never say die' attitude and couldn't fathom the idea that our precious DJ would not survive. Edinburgh Sick Kids Hospital turned into an unwanted second home for our family.

Braveheart was DJ's all-time favourite movie. Much like the characters, he showed us the true meaning of being a warrior. His indomitable spirit matched my mother's. To this day they both inspire me. Shayne and I wished we could swap places with our little brother. He was the baby of the family. The most innocent of us all. This aggressive tumour was ravaging his already skinny body. He was a child when he was diagnosed but matured at lightning speed into a young man before his time. I guess he had no choice. Invasive procedures, horrendous treatments and lengthy hospital stays forced him to grow up. As did being told he didn't have long left in this world as he was poked, prodded and injected. Had operations, lost his hair and had tubes crammed down his throat and nose. Ports inserted under his skin, weight loss, sickness and diarrhoea. Pulled away from his school and friends, isolated. All of it. And this was just the beginning.

Before my very eyes I watched my parents transform as their world was turned upside down. I felt so powerless again. I had absolutely no control over what was happening. Granny's mind was already regressing daily and now we had this devastation. It felt like watching part of my parents dying in front of me. Part of me was dying too. Suddenly I felt relieved that my grandad passed away two years before. It meant DJ would have someone waiting for him. This thought was frightening me though. I couldn't really lose my wee brother, could I? I couldn't allow myself to think it. I needed to upgrade from ecstasy to something stronger and more effective. Pronto.

Ecstasy was becoming more about consequences than pleasure now anyway. This was reflected in regular visits to A&E. Waking up all alone in hospital, attached to machines with drips was distressing enough. But to be dressed in clothes that weren't mine was quite disturbing. From what little information the hospital could give me, I had keeled over at a party. I was convulsing in my boxer shorts, amongst complete strangers. They called 999 and dressed me. Gathering whatever clothes they could find, they dressed me in a black fluffy fleece and some Adidas tracksuit bottoms before the ambulance took me to hospital.

That was one of my first rock bottoms. I felt completely degraded. Lying there in someone else's clothes with hospital bands on my wrists as doctors spoke to me. I felt humiliated. Full of remorse at taking up valuable resources that genuine patients needed. Of course, I didn't realise at the time that I had the disease of addiction. Three eccy pills weren't getting the job done anymore so I was popping as many as I could get my greedy hands on. This was the end result. The deeper I fell into addiction, the more unsavoury characters and places I became drawn to. No longer was partying as important as just getting a hit. Ending up with complete strangers became a common occurrence. No big deal.

My final fling with eccies culminated with nearly dying in hospital. My transition into cocaine began with a Tiesto trance gig. Two guys I knew who were up and coming coke dealers recommended this conversion to cokehead. I used to buy eccies from them too, but cocaine was the new flavour in town, swarming into Livingston like a party-drug plague. I would come to learn that it was much more expensive, financially and otherwise.

George and Ricky were a double act with serious connections. George was tall with long brown hair and Ricky matched his height and had short blonde hair. They also had matching swaggers and drove around in cars that screamed out 'drug dealers on wheels'. George and Ricky were well liked. I loved them too. They were proper characters. We had some great times together. They were just young lads the same as me, trying to become somebodies in a town where options were limited. Of the two, I was closest to Ricky. Taking them up on their offer, I purchased a gram of cocaine for £40.

Leading up to the gig, me, Shayne, Div and another guy we called 'Ferret' drank excessively and indulged on cocaine. Ferret brought his own stash of charlie too.

Drink-driving us to the gig was Ferret. I'll admit I was terrified as he was speeding up to 100 miles per hour, buzzing off his tits. Much like my first experience with speed, cocaine wasn't hitting me very well. Paranoia, anxiety, extreme alertness and worry was overwhelming me. I could feel the eccies in my pocket and this made me feel safer. Out of nowhere, a car caught up alongside us and challenged Ferret to a race. Ferret, a mechanic by trade—seeing himself as a Vin Diesel impersonator from a scene in *The Fast and the Furious*—duly obliged. He began racing our equally insane counterpart in the opposite motor. Whizzing along the dual carriageway our counterpart lost control. The car flew into a wheelspin, smashing against a roundabout instantly writing off the car. By the grace of God no one was hurt.

Approaching our car as we pulled up alongside the crash scene, the driver asked if he and his friend could get a lift to the Tiesto gig with us. Minimising consequences is a typical addict trait I was familiar with. Though I had no idea if this guy was a drug user or just a wild youth. Prioritising the gig over the consequences of his actions was something I could relate to. Laughing like lunatics we sped away and left them marooned there on that grassy roundabout. Whether what happened next was karma or just further consequences of my addiction, *probably the latter*, things were about to get sinister.

Pouring down with rain, the gig was overcrowded and understaffed. Security gave no fucks about people crushing into each other. I had been to many amazing raves before, with whistles and glow sticks, eccied out of my face, having the time of my life. But this was different. Cocaine had really taken effect now. My paranoia was through the roof. Time to swallow my eccies. I gubbed them all down in one. Finally, we made it into the industrial warehouse to see Tiesto perform. Excessive beats penetrated our eardrums, pounding so hard the sticky, alcohol-soaked floor beneath us vibrated right up our legs. Lasers flashed in all different colours as the crowd chanted in their finest Scottish accents: "Here we, here we, here we fuckin' go!" in unison like a drugged-up choir.

Vibrant colours shot past me as people danced around techno lasers with their hands in the air. My eccy dunt completely dropped without warning. My hands and feet felt like those massive foam fingers you get at sporting events. Lethargy was hitting me in spades. I felt so weak I had to hold on to a pillar to stop from falling to the grimy floor. This wasn't gouching. Everything felt in slow-motion. Like I was about to die. Sweating profusely, my heart started to bounce around my chest like a pinball. I started to black out. I couldn't hear the music. Only an undertone of scratchy, crackling distortions. I felt fucking bleak man. I could barely walk. Noticing my trepidation, Shayne urgently phoned Cassie to come and get us out of there. Everything blacked out. Ambiguous memories of spewing out a car window on the motorway are all I can recall. I vaguely remember Cassie holding onto me. Then I woke up in hospital.

I was attached to drips yet again, with hospital bracelets in tow. Grey paper buckets next to me were filled with putrid black liquid. My beloved Buckfast spewed up with the rest of my guts. Cassie, as always, was by my side taking care of me. She mothered me whilst my own mother had to help DJ fight for his life. Shame and guilt ridden, here I was being told by doctors I was lucky to be alive. The cocktail of drugs had done me in. Like a helpless baby I just lay there crying. It was here I first began to question why I kept doing this to myself. It was also here that I made the decision to substitute one drug for another. Eccies were clearly my problem, but cocaine would be fine, I assured myself. More than happy to eat up my own bullshit. How foolish I was again.

Vanquished from my battle with ecstasy and in denial over my brother's rapidly depleting health, my mental health plummeted. My behaviour towards women became appalling. I got into relationships I wasn't emotionally ready for. I would regularly end them without a reason. Then I'd enter them again, also without a reason. Sometimes I would break up with a girl just to see if she would cry. I gained reassurance that I was worth something of value in the cruellest way. I was also rejecting them before they had any chance to reject me. It was deplorable behaviour on my part, and I didn't understand why I was like that.

Simultaneously I was robbing Cassie of a genuine, caring relationship. At times I manipulated her to suit my own needs. I knew she loved me. Therefore, I knew she would give me lifts in her car, cook for me, support me emotionally and even support my drug habits financially. I could tell her I didn't want a relationship whilst still reaping the rewards of a sexual partner. Cassie was my crutch and my treatment of her was shameful. I didn't truly love myself either though, which is no justification. Unable to function in a relationship I re-engaged with my sexual addiction, facilitated by the Internet again.

Profile Heaven was the first dating site or social media platform where I recall people used real pictures of themselves. Paired up with MSN, I began chatting to girls online. Strangely though, my behaviour took an abnormal twist. It was common for people to ask for feedback on their pictures. I started a game I refer to as *The Fit or Minger Game*. I would pick the worst picture I had of myself and send it to women. I would ask if they thought I was fit, average or a minger.

When a girl replied fit, I felt disappointed. If a girl told me I was a minger, I felt electricity surge through me as my heart palpitated with excitement. I was instantly hooked. The next stage of my self-harming, degradation-seeking began. This developed into buying mobile phone cards in exchange for women treating me like shit online. It absolutely *had* to feel real. If a girl complimented me during the 'game' it totally killed my buzz. Cycles of addiction often led me into a paradox like this where I sought out pain for a soul that craved love and healing. This ritual developed into another unhealthy obsession.

Contradicting this was how upset I felt by how atrocious my appearance had become. Grey skin, matted hair and dead in the eyes. I was painfully thin with a sunken in face. My teeth were in a bad way. I had been headbutted outside of a nightclub when I was too inebriated to defend myself properly. Some of my teeth were smashed. The root in one of my front teeth died, turning it black. With all my money going to drugs, I couldn't afford treatment to repair the damage. I stopped taking care of myself.

As I described, my first experience with cocaine was largely harrowing. It would be absurd to go back for more, wouldn't it? But compulsively going back for more became my pattern of behaviour. Especially as I was an addict that didn't yet know I was addicted. The second time I took cocaine, just before I turned nineteen, was not like the first experience at all. This time it felt like a personal trip to heaven!

Mid-treatment, my parents surprised Declan and his best friend with a trip to Blackpool. It was the least he deserved after bravely battling his catastrophic illness with little light at the end of the tunnel. I had an empty, so I invited my mate Colin over for a party. Colin and I had started hanging out a lot more since school as we hit the party scene. Skinny, pale and blonde like me, his appetite for substances matched mine. Two-person parties are boring, so we went all out and invited everyone, including George and Ricky. Cocaine was soon on my mother's kitchen table and I decided it deserved a second chance. Crystallized white powder was spread out using a debit card then chopped up into neat lines. Rolled up twenty-pound note in hand, I snorted up that line like a hoover and fell in love.

To the sound of 'Lola's Theme' my head exploded with fireworks of dopamine, serotonin, fucking whatever! I didn't care. I was flyyyyyyyying! My face was numb, and my mouth felt like it had been anaesthetized by a dentist. Pain? What pain? Pain didn't exist anymore. I was in love. As Savage

Garden put it, for cocaine, I was 'Truly Madly Deeply' forever in love.

The sun was blaring, the ice-cold Stella Artois sliding down my throat as if it were the best thing I'd ever tasted. Colin and I were so high we were kissing each other's forehead. Suddenly George and Ricky were my fucking saviours for bringing this Godly ingredient to me. Tingling all over, I felt like I had just woken from a nineteen-year coma. Every single fucking bit of pain I had ever known was completely gone. Why on earth had I wasted so much time on weed, speed or eccies? On every one of those other drugs I felt out of control. On cocaine, I felt like superman. No hallucinations. Just a superhuman version of me. Utter paradise.

Like an illusionist, I tricked myself into forgetting all the previous consequences of substances. I owned a purple Volvo once. I had no licence. In an alcohol-eccy induced phase of madness I stole my own car, before bringing it home and reversing into my neighbour's garden. Then I panicked and ran away from home. That was forgotten. I had my nose broken when I was assaulted one night. I was too wasted to defend myself. That was forgotten. Then I needed surgery to have my nose fixed back into place. Forgotten too. Being too wasted to identify the culprit in court was also forgotten. Or how about regularly falling asleep outside overnight in children's play parks? Nope, that was gone from my mind too.

From this romantic love-in Colin and I were having with cocaine, came an epiphany. "Colin, we're both nineteen now, how do you feel about the idea of having our own place?" I suggested hopefully. Lighting up with a spark, he replied,

"Mate, I was thinking exactly the same thing! That is too crazy man. It's meant to be, let's do it!" I really gave no thought to throwing myself back into what would inevitably be another party flat, much like the house in Deans. This would ultimately be three different addresses over three years. Don't get me wrong, we had some wild times. Unforgettable times. Everyone knew where to go for a wild party in Livingston. But we ran up thousands of pounds of debt and got into wars with drug dealers. By the end we spent most of our time twitching through curtains and looking over our shoulders. But I will get to all of that.

Declan was rapidly getting more and more poorly. I was finding it hard to invest myself into anything worthy at all in life. I had no reason to believe the world was a good place anymore. The only thing I believed in was the plan to move in with Colin and keep taking cocaine. Cancer was killing my wee brother and addiction was killing me. The next three years would take me to depths of insanity I had never been to. These dark years were fuelled even more by my brother's final battles with cancer. Before valiantly falling with his sword and shield, the way he always wanted to go out, fighting until the end.

Chapter Six:
Intertwining Injustices

Colin and I moved in together as DJ's battle with cancer continued. Neither of us could cook nor take care of ourselves. We both had jobs, but we drank and took cocaine often. I began working for a large corporation in another debt collection role and Colin had a local factory job. Cassie would pertinently stress her concerns to me, "Babe, you're drinking far too much. I'm worried about how much coke you're taking too. You need to calm down."

Deluded and offended I would reply, "For fuck sake Cassie. I'm working. I'm nineteen. Fucking leave me alone. My brother is dying! I'm just trying to have a bit of fun. Does that make me a monster?" Easy for me to be so obtuse when Cassie was feeding me, maintaining my flat and giving me lifts to work as I stunk of vodka. Worse still, she was paying off tic bills for me as I spouted false promises of paying her back. Tic was something new I had discovered. Instant gratification now, pay later. Act now, think later. See the patterns?

I genuinely believed I was simply partying and having a good time. I put Derek to the back of my mind. He had disappeared from online chats for over a year now and it gave me temporary relief from analysing it. Heartbreakingly, my brother was going through horrendous experiences whilst my granny was rapidly losing her mind. Sometimes our family— particularly my mother—was going from DJ's hospital bed to my granny's hospital bed as she too was hospitalised often. Grandad dying had caused granny to get *so* mentally unwell even DJ being diagnosed couldn't snap her out of it. I needed my granny and my mum needed her own mother. Instead, Granny became like a vulnerable infant for Mum to care for.

Many tragic experiences were happening at the same time for both my brother and Granny. DJ was unable to eat much and had to be fed through a tube into his stomach. This happened at home with a machine that ran through the night. It was an alien-looking thing. The hole in his stomach could get infected easily, just like the port under his skin, leading to hospital stints. Or he could become neutropenic. Meaning his immune system was compromised due to the chemo killing off his good, protective blood cells as well as the malevolent ones. When this would happen, he had to be rushed into hospital for life-saving blood transfusions. Sometimes he was ripped from the safety of his bed in the wee hours of the morning which was distressing. Even having a temperature for a common cold meant hospital observation for at least 48 hours so he could be monitored and treated accordingly.

I could find myself suddenly sitting in the children's cancer ward in Edinburgh, surrounded by poorly little children with no hair. Some screamed in pain as I watched my beautiful baby brother looking haggard and exhausted. It was traumatic to see him with no hair and tubes going into his body. From here I would then travel to St John's Hospital in

Livingston to visit my granny. She was so poorly that she would just lie there, completely vacant. Sometimes she would stare through me like I wasn't there. Even whilst I updated her on DJ. Her grandson that she had once doted on.

My wee Irish granny used to scoop me up in her arms as a child. She would dance around the living room singing country songs to me in her broad accent. She blared 'Achy Breaky Heart' by Billy Ray Cyrus often. Yet now she would stare right through me like I was invisible. Watching my family suffer made me suffer too. I sought out my pain relief to cope. A simple text to George and Ricky saying: "3 grams on tic for 2 weeks?" would solve my problem. Then the anxious wait for a reply, and the eventual relief. "No worries mate will post it through yer letter box." This would become my predictable coping response.

Granny's health was propelling her into an abyss of madness. She was doing crazy things such as turning up at nightclubs wearing skimpy clothes and saying to people, "Let's get a shag." Or walking around handing out wads of £50 notes to strangers telling them, "I've just won the Irish lottery!" Shayne and I would have to retrieve her from these nightclubs as naive revellers would angrily shout at us, "Leave her alone, she's having a good time!" We tried to explain to them she wasn't well. Our granny undermined us by attacking us with her walking stick as she hurled vile abuse for good measure. In her distraught state of mind, her unforgiving illness meant that she too thought we were spoiling her fun.

The reality was that Granny was experiencing manic highs and lows due to being bi-polar. She had taken equity out on her house, getting herself into thousands of pounds of debt.

Ultimately my mum would become her power of attorney. Mum spent hours making phone calls and months sifting through hundreds of debt letters. She had to get support from medical professionals as she replied to every creditor. Mum was able to prove that my granny had no capacity for her actions. Thankfully Mum's perseverance paid off and most of the debt was cleared.

My mother did this right in the middle of DJ's illness. She truly is an incredible, selfless woman. Granny's illness would still find ways to hurt her though. For example, Granny would come back from unannounced trips with shopping bags full of things she didn't need. One time she came home with over fifty DVDs. She wasn't a wealthy eccentric. She was a grieving, mentally unwell widow. At a time when my mum needed all her energy to fight for DJ, she was having to fight for my granny too.

Brutal as it is to say, we had enough to focus on with DJ fighting for his life. No matter how much we willed my gran, she wouldn't mentally come back to us. We prayed hard, asking God to help them both recover. But things were getting worse for DJ. After a false reprieve with an extremely brief remission, the tumour became aggressively active again. Miracles turned into hellish nightmares once more. To my mother's disgust, we were told by DJ's doctors that all options had been exhausted. Defiantly she got in their faces and said, "There must be *something* we can do. Something we can try?"

Apologetically but matter of factly, we were told there simply was no treatment *anywhere* in the world that could save him. This news broke us all in ways I could never fully grasp. You can only ever understand that darkness fully if you

66

have lived through it. I would never wish it on anyone. It felt like we were all lost in a pitch-black world unable to see. We were all reaching out, searching, clutching for something, *anything* in the form of hope, to hold on to. But it wasn't there. Once we managed to take a breath in from that heavyweight blow, it was time to regroup.

We weren't ready to give up. DJ's courage and bravery astounded us all. We promised him we would try everything we could to get him well. It was time to make a plea on a national scale. *The Scottish Sun* did an interview with my parents and DJ. Seeing my family pleading for help in the sort of article I would usually read about other people was surreal. It tore my heart in two. This time it wasn't 'them' or 'they' it was *my* family. I wanted to take this pain away for DJ. I wanted him to have a normal life. A fair chance like everyone else. If only storylines like in the movie *The Green Mile* were true. If only some miracle man could have sucked the illness out of my brother. But this was real life. Cruel, unfair and unjust.

Good-hearted people got in touch after reading the article with ideas such as herbal teas and reiki therapies. Bless their souls for trying, but DJ needed something radical and with every new day time was running out. Something radical *and* untested came our way. Russian medical professionals got in touch with us about an untested trial treatment. It hadn't even been approved by the UK. Desperate, our family put the idea to DJ, believing he should have the final say. Like the warrior he was, DJ was boldly ready to battle with everything he had left. As a family we felt ambivalent about these trial methods.

But we were petrified and had no other options. So we defied the advice of our British doctors. DJ became a guinea pig.

DJ was no fool. He had grown into a wise young man and did not need any candid discussions about this being his last chance. He wanted to live. Russia was calling, and my family would take many lengthy journeys there for these questionable medical trials. The temperature was freezing. It was a culture shock. My parents felt distraught about everything. They didn't want this for DJ, but they didn't want to give up. DJ was even on the Russian news, almost in an advocacy role to promote this new treatment. Obliging with whatever we had to, our family just wanted our precious DJ to have a chance.

For two years this horrendous nightmare went on. During these years my addictions kept escalating. Colin and I had already lost control of our tenancy. It used to be something we joked about. The fact that our cocaine use and partying stretched into long weekends of Thursday to Sunday. Now we were making excuses to do it on a Tuesday or a Wednesday. Before long, it didn't matter what day of week it was. Most days I was turning up for work still out of my face having had no sleep. How I wasn't found out and sacked, I will never know. I was able to function as a using addict for a good few years. I was a chameleon in other environments. Personally, I believe I was given compassionate leniency due to my brother's illness.

The first direct debit we cancelled was the council tax bill. "We can catch up on that next month," Colin would say. We were completely in denial about being trapped in our compulsive behaviours. Purchasing nutritious meals petered out. Soon we were just coming home with crates of beer and cheesecakes. Maybe some beans and noodles to survive on for the month. Cheesy pasta if we were lucky. Next to fall into the well of unpaid bills was the phone bill. Soon our house phone was cut off along with our Internet connection. Paying for gas and electric became a hassle too. It was an inconvenience to our cocaine use, so that got scrapped. Debt soon piled up in the thousands.

Dreading the postman delivering mail to us, we buried our heads in the sand. Hiding letters or throwing them straight into the bin was how we dealt with this. Eventually we just let our mail pile up at the front door. Ironically, I would be at my job freezing bank accounts and arresting earnings to legally recover large debts as I dodged my own. The funny thing was, the skills I was learning in my job taught me how to avoid paying bills. Always changing bank accounts and phone numbers, I kept us one step ahead. Falling behind on rent payments is where things got messy. Less than a year in, we had to flee one address for another. It goes without saying we didn't get our deposit back. Rent arrears and leaving the flat party-worn ruled that out.

Rent arrears were irresponsible for sure. But what we decided to do next was reckless. George and Ricky dropped off a bag of cocaine one evening. It didn't have the desired effect. To be straight, it was shit. We couldn't get high. Colin and I used to always say if it smelled like lettuce we knew it was proper quality stuff, as odd as that sounds. We knew cocaine well, the way it looked, felt in our fingers, smelled and tasted in our mouths. More importantly the hit we got after taking a big, fat line. We could tell instantly we had been done over.

We snorted the contents of this little baggy. It felt like snorting chopped up cardboard or dust—no recognizable smell, bland taste and most tellingly, no hit at all. We'd bought three grams for £100. To make matters worse, a competing dealer stirred things up by telling us that George and Ricky ripped us off on purpose, taking us for idiots. They had never done this to us before. But we were buying so much we wondered if maybe they had this time. Maybe they thought we wouldn't even notice. The truth is we were too scared to ask them. We were just silly wee teenage boys. We didn't know how to contest a drug deal gone wrong.

Trying to obtain new customers, this other dealer—who I will call Carl—came over with a tester bag. The small freebie was a good fucking hit! Whilst Carl told us how George and Ricky were laughing at us behind our backs, we were getting high. A deal was struck. Three grams for £100 on tic from Carl. "Fuck George and Ricky. They aren't getting their £100 after fucking us over!" I vented to Colin in disgust. I was relieved to finally be high again.

Looking back, I truly wish I could go back in time and do things differently. I wish I had simply picked up the phone and called Ricky. He was a reasonable guy and I am certain he would have rectified the situation. Instead, when the usual tic collecting call came from George, who was a hothead, my inexperienced reply was, "What money? You are getting fuck all!" And so, a rivalry was born over one hundred measly pounds. I still regret it to this day. Truth is, we were all daft wee lads falling deeper into the serious world of drugs.

Feeling like a big shot for having 'dealt with them' I thought that would be it. Walking home from work one sunny afternoon, with the world already on my shoulders, I was caught completely off guard. A car revved up and flew down a grassy embankment in my direction! Diving out of the way like an Olympic gymnast, I watched in horror as the car skidded into someone's garden fence. About to run over to see if anyone was hurt, I saw that George and Ricky were in the car with George behind the wheel. "Holy fuck those cunts tried to run me over!" Thoroughly in shock by now, I hightailed it into some nearby woods and called Colin on my mobile, "Colin, fucking hell, they've just tried to kill me!"

I had already been carefully avoiding confrontations with Ronnie every time I bumped into him at the local nightspots. We were all a bit older and going out drinking in our respective groups. Oh yes, I hadn't forgotten about him, or Tommo. I still hated them, but I wasn't in denial over how dangerous their group was. Somehow, we had scarcely managed to avoid each other, minus the odd scuffle, for now anyway. Running into George and Ricky on a night out, however, would lead to explosive consequences.

Dancing amongst my friends, coked out of my face with a pint in hand, something caught my attention from the corner of my eye. It was an animated George with Ricky close at hand putting an arm over his chest as if to say, "Leave it alone George." Call it drunken bravado or coked up confidence but with a smirk on my face I reached out to sarcastically shake hands with George. Stupid mistake. BOOM! George violently swung his head forward smashing into my fragile nose. Like a burst radiator, hot liquid spurted all over my shirt. It overflowed from my face onto my lovely white top, staining it bloody crimson red.

Mass brawls broke out with beer bottles and pint glasses smashing, alcohol spilling everywhere. Drunken Kung Fu was no one's speciality but legs and arms flew in all directions as my group and theirs fought like rival wolf packs. Div and Colin were right in there but as usual it was my older brother Shayne going headfirst into the chaos, taking hits so that I wouldn't have to. What began as a silly £100 dispute over some shit 'ching' led to a whole variety of people—who had no issues with each other previously—threatening to end each other's lives. Bouncers piled in until we carried our brawls outside in the taxi ranks. Drunken crowds were egging on this free spectacle as if attending a UFC event. Departing in opposite directions, the insults and threats carried on as we dispersed from the club premises.

We had been back at my brother's house only minutes when they arrived in carloads. They came tooled up with weapons and reinforcements in numbers. Barricading ourselves against the front door inside the house like a human wall, we barely stopped them smashing it down. Nunchucks were the more extravagant weapons brought to the occasion, in keeping with the wannabe Kung Fu antics. Knives made up the usual hardware. I know it sounds outlandish but it's true. Admittedly it sounds like an acid trip after overzealously playing too much *Mortal Kombat*, but despite my playful description, this was terrifying.

Drug dealers are like every other employee, I guess. They had a 'boss' to answer to and the higher up the hierarchy it went the more serious a disrespectful snub of £100 was. What I am saying here is, appearances had to be upheld. We had refused to pay them and never properly discussed why. We felt disrespected by them and they felt disrespected by us. The only difference being they had some very serious people telling them to sort us out. Looking back, it all feels to me like a bunch of silly, emotionally stunted little boys trying to play at being gangsters. But in those moments, they genuinely wanted to kill us. Fortunately, one of the neighbours must have called the police which put a temporary ceasefire on the situation. But my world was getting ever more dangerous.

Another far more important ongoing war was my brother struggling to survive. Relentlessly, his tumour was overpowering any attempt by his body to recover. DJ continued to show mental tenacity throughout. Tragically, his courage alone could not defeat this rapidly growing tumour. Gruesome trips to Russia were starting to take a toll on him as well. If we carried on with the trials the consequences were potentially very grim. DJ, almost fourteen, had battled heroically for four years. Now he had to decide if he wanted to continue these trial treatments which posed risks such as going fully blind or becoming completely paralyzed. The alternative was to do what no child should ever have to. Prepare for the end of your life.

DJ had already lost sight in his left eye due to the tumour. This gave him nauseating double vision, and an eye patch to redress this. The tumour also grew through his left nostril removing his sense of smell. Radiotherapy destroyed his sense of taste and DJ often complained of things tasting like metal. He could no longer enjoy his favourite foods like macaroni cheese or spaghetti carbonara in quite the same way. As well, he'd lost his hair from chemotherapy. He had always wanted to grow it long like his favourite wrester Shawn Michaels.

By the time he had to make the decision about continuing treatment in Russia or not, he was wheelchair bound. The tumour had grown even further through his left nostril, now visible to anyone who saw him. Losing sight in his left eye was no longer the main issue as the tumour had completely grown out of his eye socket, flattening his eyeball as it grew outwards.

You may think I am describing these things as if I am somehow removed from it. Typing these words now, as my children run around playing, is the first time I have ever put these experiences into words. The truth is it ruptures my soul to revisit what my little brother had to go through. Although beyond that, it inspires me every day of my life to take positive risks and never give up. The very reason I am even writing this book is because of his example. I could never tell my brother's story and do it justice in the way my mum already has. She wrote a book about his life and journey called *DJ: Our Braveheart*, describing his legacy to us all. It was unpublished, with fifty copies made for family and friends. My dream is to have it published one day, with her blessing. I have merely provided a snapshot of some of the key moments of his journey in context with my own journey. One defining key moment was his choice about continuing treatment or not.

Sitting together as a family, we listened to DJ pour his heart out to us, "Thank you all for loving me so much and for taking such good care of me. I couldn't have made it this far without you." We tried to hold back our wails and tears to remain composed. "I don't want to go back to Russia again. I have made up my mind. I have had a great life. I just want to be at home now with my family until I go to heaven."

DJ had been asking Mum and Dad all about heaven and if he would get there safely. What parents deserve to have that conversation with their baby boy? But of course, we understood. He had been through enough and we told DJ in no uncertain terms that he had our blessing. It was no time for grieving. We had one last job to do for our DJ and that was to love him through his journey to heaven. Palliative care was arranged with the NHS staff. We prepared ourselves to walk with him down the last stretch of this treacherous path.

Chapter Seven:
"It's Just See You Later"

Littering my mind are so many mixed memories from my brother's war with cancer. A few in particular left me with shame for years. Christmas time one year, my dad asked me to donate blood instead of gifting him anything. Blood transfusions were vital to keep DJ alive. Unable to stop using cocaine, there was no way I could give my blood. It crushed me. But I managed to avoid it through a technicality. Another one of my compulsions was getting tattooed. Blagging it, I told my dad that I couldn't donate blood due to recent tattoo work. This was a genuine restriction. My dad told me not to worry. Instead he asked me to donate blood at a later date. Moments like those shattered the self-deluding aspects of my addiction. I knew fine well I was never going to be able to donate blood. I felt like the worst brother in the world.

Raising money for my little brother led me down a path of pride *and* shame. Many people were doing what they could to contribute. It all went towards the cost of DJ's treatment in Russia. Flights alone were extortionate. Proudly contributing to the pot, myself and a friend raised around £3000 by doing a sponsored skydive. Jumping from that plane was exhilarating. In a situation where I had no control over his illness this was something positive I *could* do for him. Collecting sponsor money was different then to what it is now. This was before social media took off. There were no *Just Giving* or *Go Fund Me* pages. We collected the money using A4 sponsor sheets and a brown paper bag, which was left in a cupboard at my parents' house.

One night as Colin and I were getting drunk on plum wine, we ran into a roadblock whilst trying to get cocaine. Neither of us had money and we couldn't get tic from anyone. Every dealer we spoke to wanted cash in hand that night. Lightbulb moments aren't supposed to be shameful acts, but I had yet another misjudged epiphany: "That skydive money is sitting in my parents' house, Colin. We can just use that money and put it back when we get paid?" came my utterly selfish idea. "It's not stealing if we're just borrowing it, surely?" I said, trying to convince myself. It really didn't take long for me to justify the heinous act I was about to commit.

Using my spare key, I let myself into my parents' house. Mum was in Russia with DJ and my big brother Shayne. My dad was still in Scotland but would be in bed. Sneaking into the cupboard, I scandalously started to count out other people's hard-earned money. Money that was gifted to my little brother's recovery effort. I hadn't even noticed my dad standing there catching me in the act. He was steaming drunk as well. Like myself he was struggling to cope with DJ's illness. Furiously my dad leapt at me in a rage, "You fucking thief, stealing from your brother as he's dying!" His words stung deeply but for once I had no adequate reply in my own defence. He was right in his accusations and right in his reaction.

77

He charged at me like an enraged bull! I flew backwards into a mirror which smashed everywhere. Fumbling and stumbling I tried to explain that I was borrowing the money. That I had every intention of putting it back. No matter how I tried to spin it, this was a disgusting, desperate new low for me. My dad threw me out and told me never to return. Of course, I took the tainted treasure with me. One hundred shameful pounds. In the aftermath of it, I ended up paying back double what I had stolen. But it didn't erase my actions or heal my guilty conscience. Dad catching me was a blessing in disguise. If I had gotten away with it that night, I may have kept dipping into that bag until there was nothing left.

Often my mother and I discuss how our happiest memories during DJ's illness are entangled with our darkest, most desperate ones. Humour was most definitely our family's way of dealing with some of the harshest times. DJ was shy, gentle, creative and considerate. But he also had an outlandish, whacky sense of humour. One evening he made us all ride imaginary horses through a busy Edinburgh city centre, inspired by his favourite *Monty Python* sketch. He dared us to do it on our way to see *Little Britain Live*, combining two of his favourite types of comedy. We all loved to tease Mum for being obsessively clean in the house too. So we really enjoyed a silly string battle in the living room one evening. DJ took his chance to spray her lamps, couches and even the family dogs. Even in all that pain and anguish we had moments with tears of joy and laughter.

Kindness from others astounded our family as well. Celtic Football Club invited us all to the stadium where we met star players such as Shunsuke Nakamura. DJ's primary school made sure he was at his prom with his best friends. DJ had his bandana and eye patch on and was dressed up smart. Despite having missed most of his final years of school his friends tell me he was treated like a VIP that night. They said he smiled all night. DJ adored his friends and it was a touching gift for a dying boy.

What stands out most to me is what WWE (World Wrestling Entertainment) did for him. We had written to see if we could buy tickets to an event they were having at Ingliston (where Grandad used to take Shayne and I to market). We explained that DJ didn't have long left. DJ had a bucket list and seeing a live WWE show was his number one dream in the world. Especially if Shawn Michaels was performing!

Unexpectedly we received a box full of free goodies including signed pictures, toys and DVDs. Believing we were too late to buy tickets we took that as a consolation prize. Then one day we received something magical in the mail — four free tickets to the WWE show, compliments of wrestler HHH (real name Paul Levesque). Ironically HHH was my favourite wrestler. DJ was so excited he couldn't contain himself. I cannot explain how amazing it was for our family to see DJ experience something so joyous during those horrific times. We counted down the days. DJ, his best friend Brian, Shayne and I would go to see the event.

Upon arrival there was a gentleman wearing a lanyard waiting at our seats. We were right in the front next to the ring! DJ was looking so fragile. He had his bandana on, eyepatch and a tube up his nose. But nothing was stopping him that evening. WWE's surprises kept on coming. We were taken backstage and seated in a waiting area surrounded by a four-way curtain. Sitting in anticipation, we were starstruck when HHH walked through the curtain and sat down beside DJ. We had grown up watching WWE, so it was the equivalent of meeting a movie star for us. HHH told us when he heard about DJ he had to do something. Keep in mind this was no PR stunt. There were no media around and it was before social media. This had been arranged purely for DJ. HHH looked at my brother and said, "So I hear Shawn Michaels is your favourite wrestler, huh?"

Curtains parted and in walked Shawn Michaels! DJ's dream had come true through the kindness of WWE. Emotions were overflowing. I am welling up recalling it as I type this now. Other wrestlers must have caught wind because soon we had many stars coming in to see us—Chris Jericho, Ric Flair, Edge, Dave Batista (now a movie star in films like *Guardians of the Galaxy*), William Regal, Kane and many more. In fact, we even met Chris Benoit who was so gentle with my brother that it is hard to imagine he would go on to murder his wife and child, then kill himself years later. What the WWE did for my brother that day will live on in our family's hearts forever and we will always be grateful. They made a dying boy's wishes come true.

Another powerful memory is for me tinged with both pride and shame. In DJ's final months in this world, we knew that every day could be our last with him. In the build up to Christmas 2006, DJ had been sleeping for 48 hours at a time and we were on constant tenterhooks. That Christmas Eve, Colin and I went to a local nightclub. Texting Carl, we asked for two grams of cocaine on tic. Within minutes the usual reply came to say it had been posted through our letterbox. By now we were living in a small cottage next door to a pub. Our decision making as ludicrous as ever. Returning to the cottage we wasted no time in snorting cocaine as we blared music until the early hours of the morning. I had no plans for Christmas Day as DJ had been sleeping through the previous few days. To my shock and horror, Shayne texted me at 6.30am to tell me DJ had woken up and wanted to celebrate Christmas. Shayne said he would come around to pick me up within thirty minutes. Panic kicked in.

I should have been jumping for joy. DJ had woken up and I knew in my heart he did it for our family. That was his gift to us, to give us all another Christmas together. Cocaine was pumping through my body. My thoughts were racing. I had cotton mouth. My heart was beating so hard I thought it might explode out of me like a chestbuster from the film *Alien*. When my brother texted, I was still snorting lines. There wasn't enough time to straighten up. I would purely have to wing it. With blurry vision and a pounding head, the car journey to my parents' house was hellish.

When I got there no one noticed. Everyone was just so full of joy that DJ was awake. To share Christmas with him was another miracle moment. I hugged my wee brother tight. Then I tactically sat on the couch out of view as we watched him open gifts. I was so fucked that I thought it best to keep quiet. But every now and then I tried to get words out and take part.

Every time I attempted to speak I stuttered incoherently, too wasted to make any sense. After all the gifts were opened, my mother suggested I go for a lie down in her bedroom. I did exactly that. I lay there convulsing. The comedown hit me hard as I withdrew from the cocaine. I could hear my family downstairs. Shame, guilt and remorse consumed me. I simply couldn't move. Aided by some more alcohol, I *was* able to make it back down for Christmas dinner, before making my excuses and going home to pass out. That was the last Christmas I ever spent with my little brother. It haunted me for many years that I was too wasted to appreciate that final gift. I was proud of his courage and ashamed at my lack of it.

To this day I still can't look at the pictures of my twenty-first birthday party which took place two months after that Christmas experience. I look gaunt, emaciated and dead in the eyes, a true reflection of someone in active addiction. Twenty-first birthdays are meant to be a milestone. For me, it was just another day closer to death. I used to feel reassured every night as I fell asleep in the dark, dingy bedroom in our cottage that one day I would die, and my life would be over. That was sincerely all I hoped for in life. To be relieved of it and die. I begged my grandad to come for me after DJ. Six weeks after that dreadful birthday, my beautiful brother made his journey to heaven.

Whilst watching another of his favourite TV shows, *The Simpsons*, and eating a doughnut, DJ's tumour haemorrhaged. Shayne and I raced to the house together. We were met by my grief-stricken parents and a palliative nurse. My dad had dried blood on his face from carrying DJ and laying him down on his bed. I thank my *Higher Power* that I was somehow drug-free that day and fully in the moment. We lay next to DJ, talking him through his final hours as his breathing laboured. We promised him it was safe to let go and that Grandad would come for him and show him the way to heaven. We told DJ we would all look after each other and we emphasized how overwhelmingly proud we were of our warrior.

In another *Higher Power* moment of profound spirituality for our family, DJ winked from his good eye four times. One for Mum, Dad, Shayne and me. Then a tear rolled down his face as he took his last breath. DJ had made his journey to heaven. I must be brutally honest here, I feel like part of us all went with him, specifically my parents. He passed away on Mother's Day. We believe he held on for our mum.

After a few hours of lying with my brother, Cassie came for me. We stopped at Asda to get beer. I needed it. As she popped in for the beer I broke down, crying violently. I was repeating these words over and over: "Oh my God, how can I live without him? Oh my God, oh my God, oh my God." I shook back and forth crying until Cassie spotted me and ran back to the car. She just hugged me as it all flowed out.

We drove to my cottage and sat on the living room floor with a duvet and pillows. The TV was on as Colin sat there shell-shocked. I couldn't bear to sleep in my dark bedroom that night. I associated it with comedowns and withdrawals. Cassie spoke softly to me, reminding me of all the good things I had done to support my brother.

Cassie reminisced about when DJ couldn't taste anything and we went shopping all over the place filling up a massive cardboard box full of sour sweeties. Sour sweeties were something he grew to love because it was one of the only things he could taste properly. Or how I went and bought him smart clothes because he loved to look good. Including beanie hats when he lost his hair. She reminded me how close I had become with him. DJ and I had spoken often about his illness

83

and about life. I had gone from being a brother he would argue with to a brother he could confide in. Cassie also reminded me of the times Colin and I would invite DJ over and do crazy things to make him laugh and cheer him up when he was feeling isolated and low. Basically, she reminded me I wasn't a total shithead brother, coked out of my face all the time. I loved my brother and showed it whenever I could, despite my drug abuse.

When DJ's body came home to my parents' house, I decided to sit in his bedroom and write a poem for him. Influenced by all his precious belongings—including an array of computer games, posters, clothes and drawings he liked to do—the words flowed out with ease. After completing it I went downstairs and read it aloud to my family as my wee brother lay there in his coffin. Tearing up, my family were in awe of my words. My dad stood up, hugged and thanked me, telling me he was proud of me. Finally, a moment for us to share as Dad and son. How tragic that it came under those circumstances. So proud he was, that he offered me the honour of reading my poem as DJ's eulogy at the funeral. Without a second thought I accepted. It was the last thing I could do for DJ.

The 18th March 2007
That was the day you made a journey to heaven
It broke all our hearts, you are so loved
But now is your time to rest up above
Declan J Martin, with your big blue eyes
You fought your illness, you fought not to die
How could a boy your age be so strong?
You laughed through this illness, all the way along

Always happy, you became Mum's best friend
Making her laugh, right up to the end
Your Mother's Day card, it was so true
Her character has reflected, so well on you
Mum's sense of humour, deep morals from Dad
With a Dad like ours, who could be bad?
You did us all proud, as you got on with your life
You fought like a warrior, through your troubles and strife
Your dog Louie, your collection of games
They miss their owner, it can't be the same
One thing we know, is you are so loved
Our warrior Declan is on an adventure above
You are our DJ, there is no one greater
This isn't goodbye, it's just see you later

Respecting DJ's final wishes, we gave him a send-off fit for the warrior he was. We had a horse and carriage escort the wee man through Eliburn with everyone walking behind clapping. His best friend Brian was in the family car with us. We played the theme from *Braveheart* as we carried my brother to his final resting place. Having Catholic parents, we had a traditional Catholic service and I was able to read my poem as his eulogy. Completing DJ's final wishes, he was cremated as he wanted to go out "like a Viking warrior". Like a Viking warrior he lived and like a Viking warrior he journeyed to heaven. Adrenaline and the desire to honour DJ carried me through. It was the aftermath in which the true battle began. At this point I only knew one way to cope and that was self-medication. Descending further into madness, I carried on with my volatile dual addictions.

Chapter Eight:
Into the Abyss

After my brother died, the following three years were a blurry, chaotic mess. Following in my granny's footsteps, I was losing my mind and entering a world of insanity. I was taking cocaine so often I could barely snort it anymore. My nose was constantly clogged up with hardened, white powder. It was like cement in my nostrils. Bewildered and confused, I could no longer tell what was real. Like a zombie I would walk around at all hours looking at the buildings in my street, believing they were made from cardboard. Sometimes I would stop and stare at them. I was certain that someone would pull them down in front of me. Then they would tell me this life of mine had been a sick experiment like the *The Truman Show*. I couldn't comprehend that this was *really* my life.

Mice started to frequent our cottage as Colin and I completely gave up on hygiene. In fact, it became a deranged form of entertainment. We watched the mice run from room to room, eating old crisps. Food was left on the un-hoovered carpet amongst drug paraphernalia for weeks at a time. Rubbish piled up in every room. So did filthy dishes that glued themselves together with mould from leftover food eaten months before. Flies swarmed the kitchen and unopened mail transformed into a paper tower beneath the letterbox at the front door. Whenever leaving the cottage we had to squeeze out the front door due to the amount of neglected mail. Moving the mail would mean acknowledging it. Acknowledging it would mean thinking about how much debt we were in.

Overdrafts, credit cards, large loans, small loans, payday loans and tic debts. Rent arrears, council tax arrears, phone bill arrears, gas and electric arrears. Money owed to family and friends and so it continued, on and on. By now we owed tens of thousands and still weren't paying our regular bills. Any time we had to face up to something we ordered more coke on tic to numb the pain and went to the pub next door. We got good at juggling dealers. Money was getting tight, so we began taking cheaper drugs too. Back on the speed, eccies, weed and valies. We had a few attempts at crystal meth, and I found myself smoking unknown substances from foil. I didn't even bother asking what it was anymore.

At times it could be a paradox. Colin and I would have some of the funniest times together. Everyone in Livingston knew where to go for wild parties. We loved it and became well known for it. There were times when we smashed picture frames over each other's head just for a laugh. Or random events like when a guy pulled out a gun, and everyone proceeded to the woods to shoot at trees.

When a three-day binge would come to an end, we would take a crate of beer down to a 'tarzy' by the local river and just drink. One time I came home to find Colin so drunk, he had lodged a full pint of beer on to an ironing board that was positioned diagonally. The pint was about to fall, and I asked

Colin in disbelief, "What's the fucking point in doing that?" And he replied, "What's the fucking point in not doing it?!" Another time he was again so inebriated that he kicked the living room door open as I lay on the couch gouching. He was naked and came and fought to take my pillows. He said he needed to take them "for a shite" and he disappeared into the toilet.

Despite these being some of my darkest memories, I also laugh when I look back at some of our antics. One time Colin and I fell to the floor laughing so hard we cried our eyes out. To this day, neither one of us can remember what had been funny. When we speak honestly about it though, we know that we were both completely fucked. Surviving day to day, we couldn't afford to buy food and I had already bled Cassie dry from all my tic bills.

Returning home after two days of excessive binge drinking, I was so hungry my stomach groaned in agony. Even the copious amount of alcohol couldn't numb the feeling. Desperately I got down on my hands and knees to search through the rubbish. I knew fine well my fridge and cupboards were bare. I found the treasure I was seeking. A few days earlier Cassie had treated us all to KFC. Finding a few bones with scrapings of chicken left on it, I spared no time for thought as I threw them in the microwave. Once they were heated through, I sat on the floor all alone in the dark, crying my eyes out. I looked at my derelict surroundings whilst I ate the tiniest smatterings of filthy old chicken. I had no idea how to get out of this. I truly felt my life was already over in my twenties.

I wasn't showering, washing or brushing my teeth. I wasn't sleeping or eating. People would literally stop me in the street to comment on my weight loss. Colleagues at work started to notice me turning up wasted. They also noticed when I was disappearing from the office. Sometimes it was to use coke. *Sometimes* I even went back home to masturbate. Amphetamines like cocaine fuelled my sex drive. For a sex addict like me this intensified my depravity. In turn this fuelled my shame which led to even more secrecy. I became like a helpless fly tangled up in a spider web. My sexual addiction was about to ramp up again but not before I went through a phase of diagnosing myself with a variety of illnesses.

This cycle of crazed conduct began with me blacking out at my office desk. My face smashed into the keyboard. First aid was administered, and an ambulance called to my work. My employers were extremely supportive and again they gave me the benefit of the doubt. They knew I had just lost DJ.

Fortunately, my employers provided me with free private health care. I was appointed a psychologist to work with from The Priory. In another *Higher Power* moment, this Polish psychologist came into my life right before I could kill myself, which was my next plan.

Having private health care meant I was able to access all kinds of specialist support. I never considered the fact that I was filling my mind and body with a plethora of mind-altering chemicals. Instead I self-diagnosed with an assortment of disorders and illnesses. Brain tumours, testicular cancer, chronic depression, bi-polar disorder and epilepsy, to name a few. Epilepsy was first because I kept passing out and having fits. Once I had completed hours of rigorous tests with neurologists to find out I wasn't epileptic, *much to my disgust*, I moved on to cancers. Part of me was desperate for someone to tell me I had a certain illness, to explain all my crazy behaviour. I also fantasised that if someone could just give me a pill to take every day, it might fix my broken mind.

My behaviour was beginning to really scare me. I was having conversations with myself in the mirrors at home. I even began making faces at myself and shouting out inconceivable noises as I stared at my reflection. I didn't recognise who was staring back. My existence felt bereft of meaning and the pain in my heart so deep that I couldn't bear thinking about it. Someone once made an unkind comment at a party about my appearance saying I looked like "a vampire" and this set off a new pattern of behaviours.

Obsessively I began staring at myself—hundreds of times a day—in mirrors. At home or reflections in shop windows, car windows, everything. Self-loathing each day, I became engrossed with my appearance. I would try to look at my face and body from all different angles without settling until I found an angle that made me feel better. Then if I *did* find a good angle, I didn't believe it and looked again until I saw something that looked grotesque. If I saw something grotesque, I found that easier to believe than me looking good. My teeth were the biggest issue.

I was given the all clear for the likes of epilepsy and cancer. I kept on with the psychologist though. He explained to me that I had experienced trauma through the loss of my brother. His amazing support was *just* enough to stop me from ending my own life, but it didn't affect my behaviours.

With our Internet cut off, I had no way to seek out the degradation I craved. Now that I felt so horrendous about my looks, I felt like I *needed* to be treated like shit. I ended up at a strip club one evening receiving a lap dance from one of the girls. I still don't know where it came from but in a drunken haze I offered her £20 to spit in my face. Not only did she comply with that act, she slapped my face as well, hard. Validating my belief that I was a worthless, ugly, piece of shit, this attractive woman was taking my money to treat me that way. After this modified lap dance, she introduced me to the world of *paypigs*.

A *paypig*, in the briefest of terms, was an underground fetish. This was a warped twist on the dynamics of a dominatrix and submissive. Emotional and financial domination were the themes. Perfect for men with no self-esteem or sense of self-worth who could pay someone to make them feel accordingly. Also perfect for smart women to make easy money. To be fair, it's actually a fetish that can be enjoyed by consenting adults who are healthy-minded. But at that time I wasn't well. It reminded me of my *Fit or Minger Game* with the phone cards, but on a more intense level.

Fully engaged in my sexual addiction again, I made it my mission to seek out degradation. I discovered *Babestation* on my TV Freeview channels. Now I could phone attractive women and have *live* conversations with them whilst I watched them on my TV. I directed the conversations to make them tell me I was worthless. I couldn't get a buzz or a 'hit' otherwise. Whoever owned these channels wisely made them premium rate numbers. They clearly knew fine well that desperate—or arguably unwell—men like me would call regardless of the cost. Regularly I was maxing out £20 phone cards in one conversation, so this branch of my addiction wouldn't last. I needed to get online again somehow.

Using all my *Del Boy* qualities, I got Colin and I back online. Searching for women who used paypigs, I found myself on websites with sex workers. I had always imagined sex workers as the stereotypical 'heroin junkies' (me still thinking I wasn't a *real* addict at this point) with no teeth, begging for business on the streets. What I came across was like social media for sex workers. Every fetish catered to. The women looked beautiful and appeared business-like rather than desperate people in the grips of a horrendous lifestyle. Appearances can be deceiving though and I was happy to believe these were not vulnerable women. My next ritual began.

I would send the same text to each woman that caught my eye. I would simply type: "Looking for a girl who will spit in my face, slap me and kick me HARD" then copy and paste it and text them all. Many of the texts I received back were in broken English. Many replied that they did not offer that kind of service. A few would say they would do it and offered their terms. This would set off the next stage of the ritual, travelling to Edinburgh or Glasgow. Once there, it became a battle within: "Don't do this, just go home" and I would walk back to the train until another thought came into my head: "Fucking just do it, it will feel *great!*" Inner turmoil over moral values conflicted with the cravings of my addictions.

Most of the time when I came close to doing it, I would bail at the very last minute and then head home feeling exhausted. Sometimes I would go through with it. This would be followed by horrendous feelings of remorse. Then a text message I received changed everything: "Stop texting our numbers," someone said. "You are the *kicking hard* guy, aren't you?" To which I would rebuff with a complete lie. Then they said: "Yeh well your number is blacklisted for timewasting so stop texting everyone." Mortified, I was completely puzzled. How could they all possibly know each other? I had no clue at that point how organised sex work was. But I was soon to get an insight on a night where I followed through with it.

With my heart skipping beats and sweat drenching me, I sheepishly began to head towards an address in Glasgow, minutes from the city centre. So many parallels can be drawn from how this felt compared to using substances. There was the obsessive thought process. Bargaining with myself: "Should I? Shouldn't I?" There was the fantasy aspect, the chase and the build-up. The exchanging of texts to negotiate a deal, and then the seedy, shame-fuelled walk to an unknown address for a 'hit'. For me, this time I was *literally* seeking to be hit.

Unlike drug use, visiting a sex worker was eating away at what morals and values I still had left. For some reason this felt more hidden, more taboo, less acceptable and more shameful than drug use. It is another reason I hid my sex addiction for so long. The stigmas and stereotypes.

Arriving at the designated address, my conscience was drowned out by my powerful cravings. Every passer-by made me feel paranoid as though they could see into my soul and know exactly what I was doing. It was too late for turning back. I had gone too far. I wasn't in control anymore. My addiction had taken over. I knocked on the door, which opened discretely and invited me into the dark unknown. Struggling to see, I followed the sex worker into a bedroom. She was an older, attractive, blonde woman who spoke broken English. She was Italian, from what I could make out, with red lipstick, a frilly, sexy outfit and heels.

She pointed to a side table. I realised that was where the money was supposed to go and I nervously laid it down. It already felt seedy. Laying me down on the bed she undressed me. In broken English she shouted, "So you like get hit naughty boy, eh?" as she began slapping my face. I felt a mixture of excitement and shame. Despite being aroused something in my soul felt wrong. Mid-performance, she began to get distracted and so did I. I could hear banging around in other rooms. Naively I assumed it was just her and I in this flat. I was mistaken. I heard a female voice from another room scream out, "Polizia! Polizia! Polizia!"

My eyes widened in shock! She began to scramble about getting dressed. In a wild frenzy I threw my clothes on. Translating Italian wasn't my forte, but I knew fine well someone was shouting about the police. That was when it dawned on me. This was completely illegal. Using drugs never felt criminal to me, but this did. I was only half-dressed, and my laces weren't even tied when I tried to flee. Panicking, this woman who had been excitedly slapping me minutes before, told me I had to hide in the back room until it was safe to leave. Then from out of nowhere another woman appeared. This one had dark hair and led me to a secluded hiding spot. What I witnessed next freaked me out.

On a wooden table in the living room — which wasn't really a living room — was a row of laptops. The screens displayed women on webcams. There were piles of money on the table too. Men's voices were arguing from yet another location in the flat. I felt sick to my stomach. This was some shady shit and I was right in the middle of it. I kept telling myself, "This isn't real, this isn't real, this isn't real." But it was real. Eventually, I was taken to a rear door and offered my money back. I didn't care about the money, even looking at it made me feel guilty. Leaving it behind I bolted from that exit with my belt still dangling from my jeans and shoelaces flapping about untied, until I reached safety. Overwhelmed with emotions, I fell to my knees and started to cry. I asked myself that same worn out question: "Why do I keep doing this to myself?"

That wasn't the last time I'd end up in crazy situations with sex workers. I had met an escort who called herself 'Milf Sally'. She was older, Scottish, blonde and sexy. One night I was full of cocaine and again my sex drive was through the roof. I had no money, so I offered her my microwave in exchange for a domination session. She politely declined. Another time I paid a busty black escort — a student nurse — using the currency of cocaine and two Rustler burgers. She specifically asked for a BBQ Rib one. I picked it up from a garage in a taxi at 07.30 in the morning on my way to see her, coked out of my tits.

Of course these are extreme examples of some of the situations I was putting myself in. Sometimes ridiculous. Sometimes hilarious. Sometimes dangerous. I genuinely believed I was just crazy and only death could cure me. Then something unexpected happened. I was on MSN Messenger one night when an old 'friend' messaged me: "Hi Aidan." It was Derek.

Shocked, yet curious, I replied: "How are you?" Derek began chatting away to me as if we were old pals catching up. Startlingly, something took over me. "Why did you meet me when I was only fifteen?" I typed. My hands shook uncontrollably as they hovered above the space bar. Staring obsessively at the screen I waited in angst for his reply. Never had I anticipated a reply in my life more than this moment. I would have given anything to have seen his face when he read my message. He wrote back: "You were sixteen Aidan." Angrily I replied: "I was fucking fifteen!" Derek responded: "No, I made sure to wait until you were sixteen Aidan."

Gaslighting me, Derek made me doubt myself. I gathered my composure: "I got the Internet just before I turned fourteen Derek. I remember it well. We got the Internet when we moved house. I started speaking to you when I began my paper round. When I ran up that phone bill, remember? I started my paper round when I was fourteen!" I felt agitated. My body was shaking. I stared and stared at that screen, waiting for his reply.

After what felt like hours, Derek logged off without replying. I still had so many unanswered questions. Just when the opportunity arose, and courage found me, he was gone, victimising me all over again. He would never log back in to chats or message me ever again. I thought that would be the last I would ever hear from or about him, but my *Higher Power* would lead me to his identity many years later.

Leaving me in the lurch like that, my sexual addiction went off in a completely different direction. I started searching for older men online using websites like Gumtree. I learned the term *Top* meant dominant and *Bottom* meant submissive. I put up ads explaining I was a Bottom looking for older Top 'daddy type' with two conditions. They had to be much older than me and be nasty and abusive. I knew I wasn't gay, so this made it even more terrifying that I was seeking out meetings with older men. Most of the men who replied were straight or 'straight acting'. Before long I met a man in Princess Street, Edinburgh. He clearly wasn't the man in the pictures he had shown me online.

He led me to a gay sauna in town. I was entering a world that was more surreal to me than anything I had experienced. Much like going to a local gym, the man paid our entry fees and we were handed a towel and shown the locker rooms. I was an adult in my early twenties at this stage, so none of the other men were responsible for my safety. They weren't to know how vulnerable I was. Being sexually submissive is a common fantasy so even the man meeting me had no duty of care. Apart from faking his pictures. None the less I was still in a scary world. Back in my trance-like 'act now, think later' state I followed on hypnotically.

Once I was down to nothing but a towel I walked with this man through a maze of dark tunnels and fluorescent lights. I could hear the grunting sound of men being sexual with each other. I had a shower as other men gawked at me. I don't know if their 'gaydar' could tell I was a fraud or if I was just fresh meat. We walked around and no one spoke a word. People were just throwing looks at one another to initiate something happening. Apparently, the etiquette was to say nothing and rely on facial expressions. It felt eerily odd. As did seeing hardcore porn on tiny TV screens in corners with blacked-out windows and hallways with doors to secret sex rooms. Everything in pitch black darkness.

Yet again I found myself in a situation where I was talking to myself internally and forming an exit plan. Reckoning that the safest place was the steam room, I sat in there. How wrong I was. I don't know if this is normal behaviour in that scene, but a young, foreign, dark-haired male stood in front of me, took out his penis and began pointing at it. The more I ignored him the angrier he got. After this, three older men approached me as I sat on a bench, removed their towels and began masturbating. One of them leaned in to start kissing my neck. This is where I had my first ever panic attack.

In a state of emergency, I experienced firsthand the true meaning of fight-or-flight. I felt like I was going to drop to the floor and pass out. I grabbed my towel and ran across the slippery floor with my sight restricted by steam. From here I scarpered to the front of the sauna building and tried to flee through an emergency door wearing nothing but my towel. Here I was again, fleeing a sexual encounter that my addiction had convinced me I wanted. Seeking out pain and degradation as a fantasy and being unable to handle reality. Just like all the years of substance abuse. I was hurting so much.

My *Higher Power* was at hand again as a kind-hearted Greek man—he recognised a Greek tattoo I had—with curly grey hair and glasses put an arm on my shoulder. "Are you OK?" he asked in a soothing voice. I knew he had no agenda.

98

By now, I could tell when someone really wanted to help me or not. I was a good manipulator myself when I needed drugs, so I knew he was genuine. Guiding me back to the lockers, he stood guard as I got myself dressed and reassured me I would be OK then showed me how to get out.

I left that building full of shame, guilt and remorse. I was confused and hated the secrecy that these sexual encounters brought to my life. I couldn't explain to myself why I would seek out sexual encounters with men after what had happened to me, especially as I wasn't gay. Sexual addiction felt like a sordid secret that I could never, ever tell anyone about. Years later I watched a film called *Shame* about a sex addict. I cried my eyes out with identification as I viewed the outstanding performance by Michael Fassbender. He played a sex addict with the same behaviours as me. It was the first time I felt like I wasn't alone with it.

It would be a fallacy to blame all of my behaviours on what happened to my wee brother. But the three years following his death were a blurry period in my life. I remember snapshot incidents like the ones mentioned here but there are many unaccounted periods of my life where I was blackout wasted. Regularly I was going out to bars and getting into violent fights without remembering a thing. Cuts, bruises and other people's recollections filled in the blanks. Violence broke out at our party houses often. Knives and bottles being pulled were common.

During this period Colin and I fled to yet another property, where I began self-harming with knives. Usually it was a cry for help. I would cut up the top of my arms and steer clear of my veins. Darkness took over eventually and on one occasion I decided to slice my veins and kill myself. I swear what I say happened next to be true as another *Higher Power* moment.

I hovered the razor-sharp blade over my veins. This time I was going to do it. Some otherworldly force outside of myself threw the knives from my hands. Even typing these words, I realise how far-fetched, out of this world, batshit crazy I sound. I know most people will call bullshit. They will think I am either lying, was hallucinating or that I am telling myself it happened to try to comfort myself, or believe, that someone (like my brother or grandad) was looking out for me.

All I can say is that I know it truly happened. I have questioned my sanity over this moment so many times. But it happened. Some power greater than myself intervened and kept me alive. I was so confused. My life was a fucking mess and I was degrading myself regularly. Incapable of quitting drugs, and losing my mind, I felt like a lost cause.

Two other very high-profile events happened in this period. Tragically, Ricky was killed in a car accident. I wasn't there so I can't confirm what happened. But it made the news. Some said it was just lads messing about. Others said drugs were involved. It could have been any one of us. Every lad I knew back then took risks and used drugs. I felt gutted that we never got to make things right.

I will always regret that we had even fallen out in the first place. I can judge him no harsher than I judge myself for being involved in the world of drugs. We both made those choices and we both made mistakes. We were all so young. He died in his early twenties, as an expectant father. Laying flowers at the scene, I said my condolences (years later I went back to the scene to make amends for my part in things. I wrote him a letter and read it to him, then burned the letter).

Some years after Ricky's death I bumped into George in a nightclub. George and I hugged it out over a pint. After the death of my brother DJ and the death of Ricky, in George's own words we had "both lost too much already." To George, Ricky was his brother. We had a shared pain now.

The other event came after Colin and I bailed from our final shared tenancy. Our windows had been smashed in due to our latest drug dispute. I moved back home to my parents' house. In another twist of fate, whilst playing *The Fit or Minger Game*, I met a new girlfriend. For some reason, Rachel liked the horrible picture I always used in this game. Like myself, at that time in her life she suffered from low self-esteem and was insecure. This developed into an emotionally co-dependent relationship. After everything she had done for me, I pushed Cassie away. Out of my life. I regret to this day the way I ditched Cassie. But perhaps it was a blessing in disguise for her, because I was about to make Rachel miserable for two years.

A *Higher Power* was already planting seeds in my life, however, to drag me away from the hell I was living. I just didn't know it yet. Recovery wasn't too far away, but I still had plenty of pain left to seek out, some of which I decided to experience on another continent.

Chapter Nine:
Canada and Home

Rachel was petite, pretty and blonde. We were both in our early twenties and lacking in confidence. So we fit together hand-in-glove and within weeks were declaring our mutual love. Had I had an ounce of self-awareness, I would have realised that drunkenly texting her: "I think you are the one who is going to heal my broken heart"—after knowing her for only a week—was a desperate attempt to fix myself. Likewise, had she had any self-awareness she wouldn't have replied: "I think you are already healing mine." Two insecure people, throwing themselves together without building any foundations. I had absolutely no clue what intimacy, trust, love and nurturing really meant in a personal relationship.

Due to my drug use, this was another blurry two years. The chaos had subdued ever so slightly due to moving home with my parents. I was eating well and sleeping better. The support of my psychologist helped me maintain my employment. Financial debt was still hanging over me, but at least I had no major bills to pay. Rachel and I even planned a trip to Australia. I had fantasies of 'finding myself' in the Ozzy sunshine.

With the help of my parents, I began saving money. Typical addict that I was though, I felt lost without the madness. I was using drugs incognito now that there were eyes on me at home. Sexual addiction was still rumbling away inside of me. Looking back I can see it was probably feelings of worthlessness. Because I was still seeking out pain. I was convincing Rachel that it would be exciting if we added other people to our sex life. Not what you might think either. I wasn't asking for threesomes with me, her and other women. I loved the idea of her making me jealous with other guys. At the time I thought she would feel like the luckiest girl ever. Getting the best of both worlds. But in hindsight I can see that it may have made her feel unwanted. Unloved. Pressured. Maybe even objectified.

Cuckolding is a fetish in which one party derives great pleasure from the infidelity of their partner. It can take many forms but ultimately it is about receiving gratification from third party involvement, something external from your relationship. Healthy, stable couples enjoy these types of fetishes in a safe and secure fashion. Rachel and I, however, weren't mature enough to contend with our own relationship, never mind bringing other people into the fold. Most of the time I just wanted her to tell me other guys were better than me. What I couldn't realise at the time was that Rachel barely felt loved by me as it was, due to my cocaine use. And this fetish only added to the lack of effort I made for 'us' as a couple. The truth is I never felt good enough for her. For anyone. I didn't feel worthy of love.

Eventually I became reliant upon the fetish in order to be intimate. The exciting, erotic, enjoyable feelings of jealousy would alternate with self-defeating thoughts of inadequacy. It wouldn't matter anyway as my cocaine use was getting out of control again. Then Rachel tried something that no one else had before. She gave me an ultimatum, "It's either the coke or me." For the first time in my life, it made me think about trying to stop using drugs. But I had no willpower. Two hours later I was snorting coke in secret at a party, with Rachel in another room.

Suspecting my not so subtle betrayal, Rachel burst in on me in tears, "You fucking bastard, you promised me! I thought you loved me? You don't really love me, do you?" I barraged her with pathetic excuses, "Baby, fuck sake. I just wanted to enjoy it one last time! Let me say goodbye to it and then it's all about you and me babe."

Immune to my bullshit, Rachel stormed off in a taxi and left me there. I chose to stay with my precious cocaine instead of chasing after her. She knew as well as I did that "one last time" simply meant *one more time*. Partying on through the night I was stunned at my choice. In my mind, I was head over heels in love with Rachel after our whirlwind romance and even *she* wasn't enough to make me stop.

Steve Jobs once spoke of being able to look back and retrospectively join up the dots of events in your life and make sense of them. Looking back now, I believe the way that night unfolded was another one of those *Higher Power* moments. Some might call it sheer luck. Either way it was the beginning of the end of my life as a hopeless addict. Not overnight I should add. What happened next was merely the seed being planted. I still had more pain to seek out. But before that happened, I was nearly murdered.

I was on another cocaine binge. Time and space felt distorted in these blackout benders. Shayne and I were dropping two friends off in Ladywell. Neither of us, in our drug-induced bubble, had noticed a house party opposite us. Descending from the house like Satan's army were Ronnie and Tommo accompanied by two equally wasted, hostile lads. One had been my friend in primary school in an altogether different life. "Holllly fuck!" were my thoughts. Four of them flew across the street at us, tooled up with poles, bottles and blades.

In fight-or-flight, Shayne and I became separated. I ran through dark alleyways between houses, moderately lit up by distant streetlights. I was panting like mad with a pounding heart and jelly legs. I ran as fast as I possibly could but they were gaining on me. With a quick glance over my shoulder, I saw they were getting closer. They screamed all sorts of aggressive and incoherent hate at me. My whole body was sandbagging, and my legs were giving way. I was fucking terrified, almost crying and preparing to die. As I ran for my life, I stumbled and tripped, skinning my hands bloody on the gritty pavement. I jumped back up and limped around a corner. I saw my only hope and it was a meagre one at that. In front of me was a thin bush, lacking enough density to fully camouflage me. *Something* told me to dive in there, that it was the only chance I had.

Diving headfirst into the bush, I hid in the thickest part I could find. Their voices drew closer. My stomach churned and black liquid spewed from my mouth—*my beloved Buckfast again*. I was frozen in fear, praying for the vomiting to stop so it wouldn't give me away. I prayed to my wee brother and

Grandad. I begged them to save me, "Please wee bro, please Grandad, please help me, I am desperate wee man, they're going to kill me." Tears rolled down my face whilst my arms and legs shook with tremors.

I could hear them. I could see their legs through gaps in the bush. Three of them were searching frantically for me and what I heard made me feel sick, "As soon as we get the wee fucker, stab him! Stab him! Stab him!" as their voices moved further away.

I could, not, move. They were searching for me further down the pathway near an underpass. Suddenly I had sobered up dramatically. I started to pray. You know, like atheists in the trenches who find God when they need Him. "Please God, I will stop doing drugs, I promise, I will turn my life around. I will change, please, don't let me die here, not like this."

After what felt like hours—my legs paralyzed with fear— I stuck my head out from the safety of the bush. It was pitch-black and silent. Derek's words came back to haunt me: "What's the matter Aidan? You look like a scared rabbit in the headlights. I'm not gonna hurt you." I felt like that scared rabbit. I couldn't hold back the tears. I crawled from the bush on my blood-soaked hands and knees, covered in vomit. I crawled over pathways and into the woods through muck and filth, crying in pain. Here once more, in my own personal hell. Coked out of my tits.

Somehow, by the grace of God, I made it home to my brother's house where I found him safe and well. He had gone back with a pole looking for them and me. I thank God he never found them, or it might have been his funeral next. A

106

few weeks later I would learn that such a statement was no exaggeration.

Weeks after that near-miss, merely yards away from where they tried to murder me, Tommo stabbed a teenage boy to death. Much like Ricky's death, I can only relay what I learned through hearsay and local news reports. They said that Tommo had been in the middle of a drug deal when some other young rival and him got into a fight. It shook me to the core. Weeks earlier it was almost me. I had always thought Ronnie was the one with the nasty streak. In school Tommo seemed quiet. Tommo was subsequently sentenced to ten years, for culpable homicide. I can't help but wonder what led Tommo to that lifestyle. And Ronnie. I'd have given anything to have sat down and spoken face to face with them about it all. But it has never happened.

Had this been a unique story in my world perhaps it wouldn't have shaken me so much. Everywhere I turned, I was hearing horror stories about lads, including some of my friends. Some were being done for murder. Some were being stabbed or stabbing others. Some were overdosing and dying. Some of my childhood mates were gripped by opiates, serving time for attempted murder or stealing from their families to feed their habits. I had heard about a lad from school surviving cancer then dying from an overdose. Another lad, who I never got on with at school, bumped into me one day. For some reason he confided in me and told me he wanted to join the army to get away from drugs. Three weeks later he died of an overdose.

I know many from my area and from my school have gone on to have perfectly happy lives. Perhaps they might see

107

things differently. All I could see was an epidemic of substance abuse, violence, 'lad culture' and poor mental health. It was sheer darkness. Perhaps I was just drawn more to that, but it was clear to me that so many had destroyed their lives and the lives of people around them. I was destroying mine too, just like my biological father Billy had done. That near-miss made me feel scared enough to go to my GP to talk about my cocaine use. I had received the 'gift of desperation' as we say in recovery.

I ended up at an organisation called WLDAS (West Lothian Drug and Alcohol Service) via my GP. A counsellor there—who I shall be grateful to for the rest of my life—asked me a question no one ever had, "Have you ever thought that maybe you're an addict?"

He had a suggestion, with *suggestion* being the key word here (I had a real mistrust of authority figures). He suggested I go to a local *Anonymous* meeting (out of the respect for the traditions of these meetings I do not state which specific one). Quite honestly, I never knew such a thing existed, I had only ever heard of *Alcoholics Anonymous* from television. I never related to the word alcoholic. I knew I had more than just an issue with alcohol. When I reviewed my life choices, this counsellor's suggestion that I may be an addict had a palpable aura of truth. Giving the meeting a go couldn't be as bad as my current chaotic lifestyle.

Turning up at that meeting was the beginning of the rest of my life. Though, as I stated already, not instantly. Oddly enough there was only one person at my first meeting. Everyone else was at a marathon that day so it fell upon her to introduce me to the world of living clean. Thankfully for me, she was full of compassion as she shared her story with me. She had been through institutions and was two years clean. She was my very first example of someone in recovery. That it could be a lifestyle and a genuine way out addiction.

Seeds were being planted. Meetings were in their infancy at the time, so I attended the two weekly meetings that West Lothian had and padded it out with meetings in Edinburgh. Self-supporting, the meetings were organised by addicts in recovery with four clear suggestions. Get a sponsor (someone with substantial clean time and recovery experience), go to meetings (where you can share what's going on with you), have a service position (such as helping to run a group, also known as your *home group*) and do the twelve-step recovery programme with the guidance of your sponsor (who will have already worked the program themselves). Attending ninety meetings in ninety days or, *90 in 90*, was the recommendation for newcomers to get a proper foundation for their recovery. Service positions were meant to teach transferrable skills such as being reliable, responsible and having humility and gratitude.

My head was whizzing trying to take it all in. I met people from all walks of life. Addicts straight off the street, middle-class doctors, stay-at-home mums, young lads, pensioners, people with disabilities, people of varying races, sexuality and religions or lack-of. It was clear that addiction didn't discriminate. Though it was predominantly people from housing schemes like where I grew up.

I listened to people sharing their experiences and threw myself into doing the same. Naively I began carrying myself as if I was cured. I wanted to sound good in front of other addicts who were clean. Trying to impress, I picked up on the terminology and lingo and said all the right things. I ended up on what we call a *pink cloud* in the recovery scene—a false sense of security and happiness, not much different from my first good hit on substances, ironically.

Pink clouds don't last long. Rachel ended our relationship after I had sucked the life and soul out of her through my drug abuse. Broken-hearted and beleaguered, I had no coping tools for the severe feelings of rejection. In a desperate attempt to win her back, I offered her marriage and children. I couldn't even take care of myself, so it was laughable really. What tipped me over the edge was when she met someone else. Probably someone who knew how to treat her properly.

Panicking with regret, I couldn't help but wonder if I had pushed her into someone else's arms. Jealousy nearly consumed me until a friend offered me a lifeline. Alan—a friend I had met in my debt collection role—realising my plans to go to Australia were in tatters, offered me the chance to stay with him in Canada where he now lived. I was about to go on a geographical of massive proportions.

Fifteen hours after leaving Edinburgh my flight landed in Vancouver. After a very unpleasant interrogation from airport immigration officers who rigorously scrutinised my six-month non-working visa, I finally met with Alan. We hopped into his Canadian style pickup truck. Alan was older than me, in his late forties, eccentric, with an eclectic taste in music. He sported long, flowing, greyish-blonde hair and had an infectious cackling laugh. The people loved him in Canada. He was like a Scottish cowboy and he loved Great Danes. He had one called Duke.

Often telling crazy jokes and wild stories (much like my grandad), he had the history to back it up. A jack of all trades and quite honestly a master of most of them too. He had been a police officer, a private detective, a florist, arranged security for bands like *Nickelback* and had been in documentaries on television. Self-taught, he dexterously played the drums. He also started his own business from scratch in Canada. During my stay there he took me out on the sites with him. We would build impressive water features such as ponds and waterfalls flowing down over large rocks. This ranged from modest to colossal against a backdrop of Canadian landscapes. In Alan I had an older friend who simply wanted the best for me. I didn't realise at the time that he was teaching me no dream was unreachable.

As we drove through Vancouver that first night, my jaw literally dropped in awe and wonder. Flurries of bright lights, fast paced traffic (including accordion buses) and colourful characters blended in beautifully with skyscrapers. Bars were filled with tourists. I noticed the gorgeous smells of coffee and food from an array of cafés and restaurants. Compared to Livingston, this was like being in a movie. In fact, *Mission Impossible 3* was being filmed right there! It all felt the way New York looked on TV. Wanderlust filled me, so we parked up and walked around. Merely a stone's throw away from the rich skyscraper buildings was an area called East Hastings. The police had cordoned off an outdoor community of sorts using cones. Within the cones were what I can only describe as homeless marketplaces with trolleys full of random items. Drug dealing was apparently tolerated within the vicinity of the cones. The disparity between the different areas of

Vancouver completely amazed me. Much to my surprise, I felt much more identification with the people in that homeless community.

Without further ado, Alan and I hit a blues bar in town where we began playing pool with what appeared to be two 'down and outs'. One lived in the spare room at the bar in return for washing dishes and clearing out rubbish. They wore shorts and army camo jackets. One of the guys even warned me not to count out my Canadian dollars in public, telling me I could get jumped. As an abrasive drunken Scotsman, I told him I grew up rough "so I don't give a fuck." Minutes later I spotted a young, rough-looking guy in a hooded top cycling about on a BMX outside the bar. Fuelled by alcohol, my radar was on point as I confirmed my instincts by asking him if he "had any". Enthusiastically he told me how good his gear was, "Man this is fucking *Hells Angels* shit dude. I'm on it now and I'm fuckin' high dude."

I was sold right there and then. I was curious about Canadian cocaine produced by the Hells Angels. Within seconds of taking a hit I ran from the bar toilets trying to hunt this guy down. He was nowhere to be seen and my nose was bubbling up with washing powder. He had fucked me over and I fell for it hook, line and sinker. Drowning my sorrows, I told my tale of woes to the two hapless fellows playing pool with us. Turns out I was the idiot—*nothing new there*—as the guys playing pool with us were genuine dealers. As soon as I told them who screwed me over, they were ending themselves with laughter at how easily I had been duped by what they described as a "meth-head". I didn't care so long as they had some, which they did.

This was the strongest cocaine I had ever taken in my life. It smelled to me like petrol and was so potent I felt like I might die if I took too much. It gave me the dunt I couldn't reach anymore with coke back home. After being in Canada for two days my new iPhone—gifted to me by Alan—was already full of dealers and drug contacts. The simplicity in continuing my addiction at the other side of the world was scarily flawless.

There was *one* difference this time. I had a belly full of drugs and a head full of recovery. I kept thinking about the meetings. As I waltzed about Vancouver coked off my tits like a spoiled, overstaying guest, an inner voice was telling me to get to a meeting. Not until I had dealt with my 'coke horn' though.

Attempting to avoid the comedown, I booked myself to visit a high-profile dominatrix in Vancouver. She was in movies online and this excited me even more. I did not expect things to go the way they were about to, however. Minutes after I arrived, having discussed my expectations from the session—in what was like a consultation—this very intelligent, considerate woman blew me away with her analysis. Truly a professional, she had no intentions of genuinely hurting anyone. She explained to me that she was used to rich men with fetishes and on occasion she would attract people like me. Continuing, she said in her Eastern European accent, "I think you are suffering from emotional malaise, perhaps from a parent not showing you love, or from a traumatic experience. Trust me. You do not *really* want to be here."

This was the first time someone challenged my sexual addiction façade. All these years of chasing sexual encounters and someone finally identified that my behaviour was driven by trauma (I'd learn years later through therapy and recovery that I was also an approval-seeker, linked to feelings of rejection.). To hear it from a dominatrix of all people was astounding.

I have no other way to view this than another *Higher Power* moment. Finally I saw the patterns of chasing lust and living vicariously through sexual encounters. It was a dose of self-awareness from the unlikeliest source. Hitting me between the eyes was the reality of my self-harming dysphoria, as Alan and I made a six-hour drive to the other end of British Columbia. We arrived in a place called Kelowna, surrounded by Okanagan Lake.

Kelowna was beautiful and as much as I tried to ignore my inner voice—*suddenly awoken in me as if I'd been in a coma all my life*—I had to face reality. I was an addict. There *was* a way out. Other addicts found recovery in meetings. The words of the dominatrix spun round and round in my head: "Emotional malaise. Trauma." I thought of DJ. Then I thought about my parents, grieving after the brutal illness and passing of their baby son, my beautiful little brother. I thought of Grandad. Granny came to my thoughts too. Thinking of her wandering around lost in her own mind broke my heart. I thought of Billy. I thought about what Derek had done to me. It all felt so unfair. "Why our family? Why have we suffered so much?" I asked God. "Why the hell are you keeping me alive?"

114

Months flew by in Canada. Despite Alan looking out for me, I was painfully homesick. Confused, I asked Alan to take me to a local recovery meeting in Kelowna. I was welcomed like a family member by all these beautiful Canadian strangers. Some of them fully in recovery and others desperately trying to get a day clean. This new inner voice was telling me to help others. Recovery teaches you about humility and giving back, so I started to volunteer at a homeless shelter in downtown Kelowna run by a Christian Gospel Mission. From the kitchen I prepared and served food to weary people who were broken like me. I identified with them like I was a long-lost member of their tribe. The more hours I put into the homeless shelter and meetings, and the less I spent in bars or waking up in strangers' basements, the more my heart felt at ease.

Torn between two worlds, I tried to successfully use drugs whilst also taste a life of recovery. Like a toddler trying to walk I needed help. My addiction was still in control. Funds were rapidly running out and I was pulled closer to the edge of insanity again when my *Higher Power* answered my call for help once more. Two guys from meetings in Kelowna had heard about me. One was an older English guy and the other a big, burly Scotsman, ironically called Billy, like my biological father. They took me under their wing. Billy and Alan knew each other, being two Scotsmen in Kelowna. Apparently there were a few of us Scots over there. We were well liked. All the Canadian girls loved my accent and always asked me to shout "Freeeeeedom!" after the *Braveheart* movie. Whereas I always found it funny that Canadian guys called everything 'her'. Such as a bottle of beer: "Drink her." And I loved how

Canadians said "eh" after everything, because us Scots do the same!

For a while Billy took it upon himself to sponsor me. He tried to help me. But even he could see I was struggling badly. One night after a meeting the English guy and Billy spoke to me. Billy said he used to be involved with gangs in Scotland. He even said he used to "run around" in West Lothian. He claimed he briefly knew of my biological father. I wept like a baby in front of these men. Just hearing him say that he knew of my biological father hit home. I was convinced a *Higher Power* was looking out for me, like it was a message. I know these *Higher Power* references might sound far-fetched, and I almost don't want to include them in this book for fear that they do, but these moments really happened. Time and again. I can't ignore them. I wouldn't be writing this book if it wasn't for them.

Leaning into me, gently but firmly the Englishman said to me, "You need to go back home son. Canada is huge, and yer gonna fall off the grid soon." Billy, my biological father's namesake, picked me up by the scruff of the neck and told me, "Speak to Alan son. He cares about you. He needs to know you're struggling. You deserve better than this."

I took their advice and spoke to Alan. With his help I cut my stay in Canada short and flew home. I had taken my addiction to the other side of the world and my *Higher Power* had found a way to save me, once again. Volunteering in homeless hostels had planted another seed in my mind. I knew in my heart this life was a wasted one if I wasn't using it to help others. Upon arriving home in Scotland, my mother and I took a walk through a field where she told me she was worried about me. She felt I was deflated since I'd gotten home. I said to her, "Don't be worried Mum. I don't know *why* but all I can tell you is I feel I've been called home for a reason." I wasn't wrong.

Chapter Ten:
Recovery

Returning from Canada was anticlimactic. It felt embarrassing having told everyone I was moving there for a new life. Failing to 'find' myself in the mountains—surrounded by wildlife as I had fantasised—I was yet to appreciate just how life-changing this trip would turn out to be. Serving food to people who had lived through hard times in Kelowna was my first taste of the intrinsic reward of selflessly giving to others. There is a saying in recovery which I feel is apt here: *We can only keep what we have by giving it away*. Because of this experience, and with my mother's encouragement, I gained a place on a three-year course studying health and social care at West Lothian College.

I was attending meetings again, and back living with my parents. Excitedly, I showed the college acceptance letter to my dad. His response deflated me. "Three years?!" he exclaimed in horror. "You're not a young man anymore son, you should be working. You didn't exactly thrive at high school." It was a crushing blow to my confidence. But my mum told me to go for it, no matter what.

College was a gift that came into my life when I needed it most. I was doing just enough meetings—*without fully committing* — to keep my head above water. I had periods of months where I barely touched substances. I was thriving at this amazing college. It was an educational environment that blew me away. Instead of teachers who looked the other way as children were horrendously bullied, I had lecturers nurturing my mind and encouraging my intellectual development. They believed in me when I barely believed in myself. Every day I was being told how bright my future could be. Every day I received positive reinforcements about my abilities. "You're extremely smart and insightful Aidan," one would say to me. "You're going to go far Aidan. I feel it in my bones," said another.

Most teachers barely looked my way in high school (apart from a couple, like my History teacher). Those lecturers at West Lothian College, however, built me up from nothing. It took me until I was a twenty-five-year-old mature student to realise I wasn't stupid. I never had a fair chance at education in high school. Lecturers even noticed my interest in crime and guided me to change course in year two to do social sciences. I would go on to study subjects I was passionate about such as criminology, sociology and psychology. I was even able to develop leadership, communication, advocacy and mediation skills as a class representative.

I was flying, but there were still challenges. Dad was pressuring me to leave college or skip years and finish early. My mother, on the other hand, was adamant I stick with it. She could see how much it was changing my life. I was still making self-harming choices though. 'Pure' cocaine arrived in Livingston. My previous cocaine at £40 per gram was now known as 'council' and thus relegated. Pure was the new brand at £100 per gram. I couldn't help but wonder if this new pure coke was the same stuff that gave me the dunt back in Canada. The obsessive thoughts trickled into my brain once more.

As I successfully flew through college, I got into another relationship I wasn't ready for. With one of my classmates no less. Kirsty was the stark opposite of Rachel. She was a tall, creative, DIY girl. She wore high tops and chequered flannel shirts and tunnels in her ears. Brunette hair and massive, pretty eyes complimented her vulnerable yet feisty character. We were both on rebounds and desperate to be loved. We had a good run to begin. But at times our relationship was erratic and became on again, off again.

Arriving at my parents' house one day, Kirsty brought a dainty little bag with a baby grow in it. I was so wrapped up in my own world I hadn't even noticed her placing it in my room. I hadn't noticed she was putting on weight either. Finally one day she spelled it out for me. Bursting into tears she muttered the words, "I'm pregnant." The shocking truth finally hit home.

Reeling in shock from the news that I was going to be a father, I slipped into denial. I told myself, "Everything is going to be just fine." Kirsty and I moved in together a few months before the unplanned arrival of our son. It felt like the right thing to do but I soon realised I was deluded. I thought we could just play happy family. But we had barely even built a relationship. We had already broken up a few times before Kirsty fell pregnant and had no foundations to build a family together. Despite all of this, I thought maybe this little baby would cure me of my addiction, or 'fix' me. It happened at a time when I was just starting to discover who I was, halfway through the college course.

Luring me still were the temptations of pure coke. I began pulling away from recovery. Watching my college classmates go on wild nights out filled me with envy. I felt I was missing out. "I'm too young for abstinence," I would reaffirm to myself. Abstinence from *all* substances is the requirement to be completely clean in the recovery fellowship I was dipping in and out of. All I was doing was self-deluding once again. We call this a 'reservation' in recovery. That is, I was keeping the door open mentally by secretly promising myself that I would eventually try this pure cocaine. My arduous battle with substance abuse was minimised in my mind once more. "I deserve a treat," I would tell myself, congratulating myself for working hard at college and managing periods of abstinence.

I managed to stay clean by the skin of my teeth. I felt like a caged animal. But the relapse finally came. It was on the day my son Caleb DJ (named after his uncle) was born. Having my baby boy handed to me should have been the best moment of my life. It *was*, but in that moment, I was overcome by feelings of dread. Reality really hit home again. Now I had someone more important than myself to love and care for. Someone who relied on me. Shamefully and disgracefully, as soon as mother and baby were home, I cashed in that reward I had been promising myself. Just like my biological father Billy had done at my birth, I abandoned my partner and child to 'celebrate'. An excuse to go and get wasted. Having always told myself I would never, ever be like Billy, history repeated itself.

Relapsing sent me spiralling quicker than I could have imagined. It was what I deserved. Despite all the gifts that came into my life I had stuck two fingers up at it all. Insanity is repeating the same mistakes and expecting a different outcome. The outcomes this time were demoralising. My precarious relationship with Kirsty finally fell apart. I became homeless. I ended up living on a mattress on the living room floor of my granny's home, where my big brother still lived.

By now Granny had carers four times a day to assist her with vascular dementia, bi-polar disorder, and partial paralysis from multiple strokes. Carers were so used to me lying on the floor convulsing, wearing nothing but boxer shorts, that they would step over me to access my granny's medicine cupboard (ironically where Grandad's tapes used to be). Next to my mattress was a cardboard box containing what few possessions I had left. I lost access to my baby son. Recovery was gone from my life, and college my only beacon of hope remaining.

I lay on that mattress desolate and empty. I realised I was beaten. Defeated. Done in. Fucked. Spiritually, emotionally, mentally and physically bankrupt. My finances were fucked again too. I decided to do the only thing I had any energy left to do. Pray. "Please God, save me. I can't do this anymore. Please just take my life and do what you want with it. I beg you." I truly meant every word this time. I'm not sure if I expected a massive beam of light to shine down on me. Some miraculous healing or something. But in a tantrum, I decided God hadn't answered. My next best plan was to 'go out' in style.

After a three-day cocaine binge, I decided to end my life. Failure as a father was staring me in the face. I had petulantly decided that God hadn't saved me. Not on my terms anyway. I had already forgotten all the times people had been put on my path to help me.

Ladywell is where it all began. So, in my romanticised fantasy, Ladywell is where it was going to end. I had no idea what time or day it was. It felt like a desperately lonely, dark evening as I staggered to a place I knew well. Standing on a bridge I often crossed as a child, I was overlooking a dual carriageway directly facing Ladywell. Opposite the bridge was the pub my mother used to work in, where she met my dad. The very pub my biological father drank in. It was the same spot 'Mad Rab' drank at with other alcoholics too. And just below me was the church I had been christened in, St Paul's. Staring down at the concrete road I willed myself to jump as I said goodbye to my past.

I didn't want to live anymore but I didn't want to die either. I just felt like I couldn't go on. It felt like there was no way out. Instead of my beautiful baby son fixing me, my failures as a father sent me spiralling even lower. My soul was torn and tangled up. My mind was damaged. My perception of love was fractured.

Failing to stop using substances for my son made me feel hopeless and powerless. Each time I tried to throw myself forward over the bridge I stopped at the last minute. This was more than a cry for help. I was trying to throw myself over but the thought of abandoning my son (as my biological father had done to me) or to cause my parent's heartache at losing another of their children, was holding me back.

Psychosis must have been in full force. My sense of time and space was distorted. In an instant I felt as if I had gone from howling blood-curdling screams, all alone on the bridge, to being surrounded by emergency services. I was too numb to take it in. Roads below were closed off and lit up by the flashing lights of fire services, ambulances and police cars. Slowly but carefully approaching me was a clean-cut, handsome looking fellow wearing a police uniform. He had his hands out in a non-threatening stance. A short distance behind him was a slightly plump, concerned-looking paramedic.

Ever so gently, this Scottish cop with a Spanish name, which eludes me, so I shall refer to as Pedro, cleverly approached me inch by inch. With each thoughtful step he simply spoke to me. I felt no pressure. No judgement or condemnation from him. Not even for taking up all these emergency resources! Unwinding me piece by piece, he somehow got me talking about my son and studies. Treating me like a human and not an addict, he floored me with his thoughtful words, "Your son needs you mate, so do other people. You didn't start your studies for no reason. You can't help people if you jump off this bridge. Finish your studies like you set out to do."

Laughing through my tears I said to him, "Oh you're fuckin' smart Pedro, you're inside my head now," and we both laughed with each other in that surreal moment. He reached out his hand willing me to take it. Letting my clenched grip of the steel railings go, I dropped to the bridge floor in a battered heap. I was relieved in one sense but terrified in another. What now? I knew something for certain though, my *Higher Power had* answered me. I was hell-bent on self-destruction and would have killed myself if not for the compassionate cop Pedro, who saved my life.

I fully expected to be taken to the cells. Pedro had been straight with me. Finding drugs in my system would mean having to arrest me. Three days of binging meant it was inevitable. The paramedic took my blood. He too treated me with compassion and dignity. Though I cannot recall the words used. I just remember feeling like a human. Pedro amazed me in telling me I was "all clear and free to go home."

Pedro spared me. Avoiding the cells, I *was* taken to see a psychiatrist at A&E where for the first time in my life I admitted to my big brother and my parents that something happened to me as a young teenager. Though I was unable to name Derek or discuss any details. All I could explain was that something had happened with an older man. After that night, I shut everything down inside my head again and refused to talk about it.

I crawled back to recovery meetings. I wanted to be a good father to my son and finish college. Most importantly, this time I *wanted* to be clean, not just for other people, but for me. I wanted to begin healing. Dragging myself back to a meeting, it happened to be a *birthday share*, meaning a clean-time birthday. Celebrating clean time was another incentive in recovery and the man sharing was two years clean. He picked up a black, multiple-years-clean-and-serene keyring and shared to a lively room full of raucous addicts. Putting an arm over my shoulder, one long-termer who remembered me said, "I still have the same number." Recovery works just like that, one addict helping another.

Ironically, Barry, the man sharing, had been a 'newcomer' when I attended meetings in the past. He was a nervous wreck when I met him back then. At the time I told him to "keep coming back" which is another recovery saying. Unlike myself, he did keep coming back and he stayed and *done the deal* (another cliché but life-saving piece of recovery terminology).

Remember those four suggestions I spoke of earlier? That's the deal. Simple as that. Recovery is open to everyone from any background and the only requirement is a willingness to get clean. Seeing Barry's transformation put me in a pensive mood. "If *he* can get clean, maybe *I* can get clean." Belief and hope entered a soul that had been barren of both.

Birthday shares are inspirational, and emotions were flowing as Barry told his story. His elderly mother was there, and I could see how much this meant to her. Barry too. His eyes welled up. It made me think of my own mother. Scanning the room, I spotted others I knew from before. John, who couldn't keep his head off the table when I last met him in a meeting, shared after Barry. He was also transformed.

Instead of the lad I met who was strung out on heroin, covered in his own blood and thick with filth, here John was clean with a passion for life. He too kept coming back whilst I was cherry picking recovery and keeping one foot in my using world. Dr Fred was there too, a middle-class friend from before who had taught me that addiction has nothing to do with stereotypes the media sells us. He was self-deprecatingly arrogant yet caring, kind and articulate. He had dragged John back to recovery from a using den, quite literally a using caravan! Dr Fred has been someone who has guided me as a friend, in recovery, in my studies and in my career path ever since.

Finally, I was ready. Picking up my white first-day-clean keyring, symbolising surrender, I began to give up Aidan's ideas of wisdom and simply listened. Stereotypes and stigmas are dangerous, I learned. I realised in past experiences with meetings I was looking for differences with other addicts instead of similarities. I had told myself back then that I wasn't a 'real' addict. I had never been in prison or treatment and had never knowingly used heroin. So it kept me away from meetings and ironically back to my addictions.

Absurd, foolish thinking like that nearly cost me my life. Thank God for the recovery vanguards who brought meetings to West Lothian to save people like me. Addiction, I was to learn, was a complex disease of the mind and soul that could be remedied with a simple, but not easy, programme of recovery. Drugs of choice (mine being cocaine and sex/degradation) are just an addict's attempt at a solution. Addiction is the problem.

The disease of addiction is a dis-ease of self. I identified with every person who shared feelings of alienation in society. A sheer inner loneliness and lack of self-worth or self-esteem. I related to that 'hole in my soul' which I continuously attempted to fill with sex and substances. I related to it all.

Spiritual malady. Not feeling comfortable in my own skin. Self-loathing. Self-defeating thought patterns. Obsessive thinking and compulsive behaviours. With each feeling, pattern or behaviour discussed my eyes widened with identification. "*How have I never taken any of this in before?*"

127

I asked myself in disbelief. Well it was simple, denial and self-delusion combined with the selfish, self-centred nature of active addiction meant I never became accountable for my using. At that point I was also just starting to understand societal reasons for addiction through my studies too. All those years I had no awareness of what I truly suffered from. I wasn't a unique case after all, nor was I crazy.

Addiction was an odious illness far more powerful than I was, rather than a moral failing of character. I had spent my life feeding my addictions instead of learning healthy coping methods and finding constructive solutions. I hadn't grown up or faced any of my feelings in life. My answer to everything had been sex or substances. No longer was I willing to live that way. That mattress wasn't going to be my future.

Asking John to sponsor me, I *lived* the four suggestions and wholeheartedly dedicated myself to recovery and a life of spiritual principles. Principles including honesty, humility, gratitude, perseverance, patience, tolerance, acceptance, forgiveness, faith, surrender, hope and unconditional love. I should highlight that you don't transform into a spiritual guru here. It is about striving to live closer to those principles as much as possible. I was still Aidan. I was just being given a better toolset for life. I know what you might be thinking. Higher Powers, group meetings and spiritual principles. Must mean a religion or cult. The reality is nothing of the sort.

A Higher Power *can* be the God of your own understanding. But it can also be the universe, your sponsor, the group meetings, a combination of them all or something entirely of your own choosing. God can mean *good orderly direction* or *group of druggies*. Dr Fred is an atheist and one of the greatest influences in my life. I'm not a religious guy either. Honest addicts will tell you that their drug of choice was their higher power for their entire using career. Indeed, I was now no longer in denial that the disease of addiction was a power greater than me. Evidencing this was my complete inability to stop on my own. Therefore, I needed some other power greater than myself to keep me clean.

Recovery is where I was spiritually awoken. I finally found a sense of belonging and identity. There is no room for self-pitying so hiding behind DJ's passing or even what Derek had done to me wouldn't be tolerated as a justification for using. Harsh as that might sound to some, it is exactly what I needed to stay clean. Recovery is about *living life on life's terms*.

Step one of the programme literally looked at my powerlessness over addiction and how unmanageable my life had become. As I worked through the twelve steps, I was able to identify how insane my life choices had been and how skewed my decision-making was. The steps, to me, are like having a therapeutic, spiritual and psychological look inside every nook and cranny of my mind and soul with the guidance of a caring sponsor *and Higher Power*.

Being humble and trusting enough to follow the guidance of others is paramount in recovery, as is the ability to get honest. Being involved in service positions such as helping to run home groups made me feel part of something. I was learning to build relationships from scratch. I would have to write another book to explain the twelve steps fully and even then, *Russel Brand has already covered this excellently*.

However, I can provide snapshots of the types of things I dealt with in my step work with my sponsor.

Together, we looked at areas such as my fears, resentments, relationships and sexual conduct. My behaviours and the root causes were analysed. We looked at the wrongs I had done to others and society as well as how others and society had wronged me. I got honest about my defects of character whilst also identifying my assets. Amends were to be made to those I harmed, *where safe to do so* (for example turning up in Cassie's life at that time to make amends may have caused her harm). I also made amends to society and to myself.

Whenever I fucked up I worked hard to identify it. When I was in the wrong I would put things right or make amends as soon as possible. Importantly it was about amending my behaviours so as not to hurt other people in the first place or myself.

Finally, the steps were a commitment to helping other addicts and giving back to society. It should also be said that recovery is not a substitute for seeking out professional support from psychologists or counsellors, etc. It would be reckless to tell a person to just join a fellowship and rule out professional support. Professional support is a big part of my recovery too. Many compliment their recovery with additional help. We are not professionally organised in a fellowship, just addicts freely supporting each other back to health. But the point I am getting at, is recovery was the foundation for me getting well.

Even though I was clean the tentacles of my addiction found other ways to branch out. I worked in retail whilst a college student. It was a high-end brand. Before long I was feeling unworthy again. I started to feel like I needed all the best designer gear to be a 'somebody'. Two of my male colleagues were body builders. Their muscles bulged from their clothes. I compared myself with them. I didn't feel like a 'real man'.

Before I knew it, I was back into my body dysmorphia and guzzling protein, casein, creatine and Slim Fasts on top of my meals as well as eating everything in sight. I was trying to fix myself and look like that 'real man' image. It became unmanageable very quickly and only made me feel worse about myself. I learned that addiction can take on many forms, whether you are free from your main source of pain or not.

War stories of lives spent in active addiction were common in meetings. But it was far more than recovery raconteurs telling tall tales. Something magical happened in those rooms and I sincerely cannot explain it. Contrary to my many *Higher Power* references I am not into 'airy fairy' concepts. Recovery is real. The more I listened the more I learned how real addiction is as an illness in society. It can branch out in many ways such as substances, sex, gambling, food, social media, clothes, money, status, ego and the list goes on and on.

With the four suggestions as the foundation, my life took off. I graduated college with flying colours and began living a life beyond my wildest dreams. I started at Glasgow Caledonian University for a degree in social sciences. I also took on a voluntary role supporting victims of crime—both in society and through criminal trials. In this role I supported victims, witnesses and family members through horrendous trials of murder, rape and domestic abuse. I learned first-hand about the criminal justice system in practice as I studied it in theory at university.

Growing at an accelerated pace in my recovery, I also began working in two homeless hostels in Leith, Edinburgh. I was able to support people struggling with homelessness, addiction and poor mental health, just like I had been. It didn't stop there. With the help of my parents I was able to pay off my financial debt (as tough as things could be with my dad, he has always had my back with stuff like this) and moved into my own tenancy. I took care of this tenancy with pride, unlike all my party houses! Most important of all, I got my son back in my life and was able to be a proper father to him.

Higher Power moments continued in my life. I made some great friends at university, specifically two friends. One was a girl called Sam who I already knew from college. She was around my age and so was another great friend I made called Darren. He had kids too and we gelled instantly. The three of us had many good laughs and supported each other through the whole journey, becoming life-long friends.

My friendship with Darren had not been built around my addiction. In fact, he proofread this whole book for me when it was simply an idea. If it wasn't for Darren, there would be no book. The three of us thrived at university with all our other friends. And I kept on learning about society and human behaviour. With each new theory or subject, I understood myself better.

At the same time, as I studied in coffee shops (coffee being something Alan introduced me to in Canada) I met a student nurse who worked in my local Costa Coffee, also called Sam. She was petite, blonde and radiantly pretty. I loved her strong, vivacious personality. We really hit it off after she mocked me for studying at a tiny table, surrounded by books. One of the things that attracted me most about her was that she was headstrong. She refused to jump straight into a relationship and took her time. Eventually we began dating and in time fell in love. I began my first healthy relationship with a woman in my late twenties (as a joke we call my partner Sam one, and my friend Sam two).

Recovery was healing my broken soul and teaching me about myself whilst university was teaching me about society. Studying gave me an awareness of the social inequalities and barriers to success that many of the people I grew up with faced. Social deprivation or social mobility were concepts I'd never heard of before. I didn't grow up in poverty, but the streets were harsh, and I know many of the lads I grew up with came from nothing. Some of them had no fair shot at life. My high school was a complete failure for me (and many others I would argue). Friends recall news reporters outside of our high school doing stories on how poor the school was.

Studying psychology got me thinking about the effect of discovering hardcore porn so early in life. About the impact of meeting Derek. How both things impacted my sexual need to be abused. I am not conflating this with domination fetishes. There is nothing wrong with a fun fetish between consenting adults. I still enjoy many of them. I just mean the desire to go further and seek out abuse. Or to seek out a fetish to the point of damaging myself or a relationship.

With Sam I was learning what it meant to be in a nurturing relationship based on mutual respect and equality, whilst being a father taught me the true meaning of unconditional love and responsibility. I had also never grieved properly for Grandad or DJ. Or faced my feelings of abandonment and rejection about Billy.

Recovery provided me with the tools to start facing these things. Each meeting would end with us all holding hands in a circle (still not a cult, I promise) and saying the prayer '*God, grant me the serenity to accept the things I cannot change, the courage to change the things I can, and the wisdom to know the difference. Amen*' (still not religious either, I promise). Not so much 'Shiny Happy People Holding Hands' as it was 'Rough n' Rowdy Recovering Addicts'. Ha! And I loved being one of them.

Inspired by my growing knowledge of the disease of addiction—with an awareness that my biological father Billy was an addict like me—I made contact with him through Facebook. My fantasy of him turning up in a leather jacket with an adventurous story didn't come to fruition. It was replaced with the reality that he was still living a substance abuse lifestyle. Apart from telling me a few songs to listen to, so I could "better understand" him, he had no interest in me, Shayne, or his grandkids. I *did* have some contact with other members of my biological father's family. Despite early impressions that they were overjoyed to hear from us, most of them made no effort.

That experience was another painful rejection. I wanted so badly to understand that part of my life. It was important for my sense of identity. But I couldn't force Billy to want me. It wasn't anywhere near as bad as what was to come, however. Living life on life's terms was the true essence of clean living and early in my recovery I was about to get hit with a curveball no one could have seen coming.

Halfway through university, with my life stable, my son Caleb—by now two and a half—had been picking up a lot of viral infections. Paranoia was consuming my mother after everything we had been through with DJ. Blood tests weren't showing up anything sinister. However, my mother would reiterate that DJ's blood tests were clear in the beginning as well. Over time I became angry at my mum for implying Caleb could be seriously ill too.

Then one day as we took Caleb to soft play, we noticed him limping. We all knew something was seriously wrong. My gut was screaming at me. I didn't want to listen to it. I was too terrified. After many more blood tests Caleb was becoming extremely poorly. One afternoon we were rushed to the paediatric ward at St John's Hospital, Livingston, for an urgent meeting.

Arriving at the ward, my mother and I met with Caleb's mother, Kirsty, and her parents. Caleb was so poorly that day it was frightening me. He looked like he was dying. Nothing was making sense. Kirsty and I were ushered along to see a specialist in a room at the end of what felt like the longest stretch of corridor I had ever seen in my life. The sombre tone of the nurse was obvious as Kirsty and I followed on like we really were walking the *Green Mile*. Kirsty turned to me unnerved and in a panicky voice asked, "Oh my God Aidan, what are they going to say?" Fearing the worst, I squeezed her hand gently and said, "We will find out together."

Chapter Eleven:
Here We Go Again

Not knowing what was wrong with Caleb was my worst nightmare. I felt completely helpless watching him deteriorate. The medication for viral infections wasn't working. One time my baby boy was lying in the bath crying in pain instead of splashing around having fun. That nightmare became real as Kirsty and I were sat in front of a specialist. Someone we had just met. His words turned our lives upside down. I went through this as a brother already. Hearing the word *cancer*. I watched my own parents struggle to come to terms with this illness when it was their child. So for me to be sitting in front of a specialist myself, thirteen years after my brother was diagnosed, felt unreal. It wasn't even the specialist who used the word cancer first. It was me.

Kirsty and I listened intently as this very polite, professional Asian specialist spoke in medical riddles. Further blood tests determined there was an issue with Caleb's blood cells. The moment he said the words "blood cells" everything froze as if a sheet of ice came over me. I'd heard it all before with DJ. Mum was right. She knew all the signs and had been so insistent that something was wrong. I had never been more terrified to say what came out of my mouth next: "Do you mean, cancer?" Apprehensively, he replied, "Yes, a type of blood cancer. We believe he has one of two possible types of leukaemia."

His reply sent me into a spin. I wanted to wake up. This couldn't possibly be real. Not again?! A few weeks ago my son had a viral infection and now this? He was only two-and-a-half for fuck sake. Just an innocent toddler. Falling to my knees, I bawled my eyes out repeating the words: "Don't tell me that, please don't fucking tell me that." My precious baby boy had child cancer just like his uncle DJ who hadn't lived to see him be born.

Kirsty cried her eyes out too. Trying to reassure us, this specialist who we had known for only minutes, kept telling us, "We can treat this, it is OK, please don't worry, his chances are very high." A clearly distressed team of people from the paediatric ward chimed in and explained that through our sheer perseverance we had caught it early. Though unlike tumours there are no stages for blood cancer.

We were told to go to Edinburgh Sick Kids Hospital, immediately, to begin tests to find out which type of leukaemia Caleb had so they could begin treatment. Somehow, Kirsty and I mustered up enough strength—amidst the furore of emotions and numbness of this earth-shattering news—to go and tell our families. Everyone was inconsolable.

By now Sam worked in the hospital we were in. She came running up in her nurse's tunic hugging everyone. We all fell into each other's arms crying. With anger and revulsion I turned to my mum and said something I regret, "There can't be a God. What kind of a fucking God would do this to our family twice?" Fearing the worst, I told everyone, "If he dies,

I am going with him." Stunned by the news, we travelled back in time to a world we thought we'd never enter again. Nothing made sense as we headed back to Edinburgh Sick Kids Hospital. We knew this place all too well.

Arriving there with my family felt surreal. I am certain the pain I felt inside wasn't disguised by my face. All I could hear in my head was the word cancer. I was in a state of panic. I thought I was going to lose my son. Recognising my mother from before, members of staff hugged her in disbelief that we were back again.

I held onto what strength I had for the sake of my son. But it was tough. So it was an enormous relief to see my sponsor, John, walk into the hospital. Sam had called him with the news. John greeted me with a loving, heartfelt hug. His presence switched my head back on. He reminded me I was in recovery now. It wasn't time to crumble. It was time to fight. I had come a long way since stealing toilet roll from pubs to survive. Now I could be the father my son needed, when he truly needed it most. Applying spiritual principles such as acceptance, faith, trust, hope, belief and surrender, I regained my composure.

The medical terminology was bewildering. Kirsty and I spoke with many medical experts who told us that Caleb's chances of survival were high. They had to determine what type of leukaemia he had and then treat it. Either way, they told us the first few months would be horrendous. Those first few months *were* horrendous. We had to dig deep and get Caleb through this as his life was still in danger. Never had I been more grateful to be clean and in recovery than I was now.

Being present in the moment was more important than ever and I gave Caleb everything I had.

I wished I could have swapped places with Caleb. Take all the pain for him. But fantasy was no good. So I surrendered to the situation and accepted our reality. I kept faith in my *Higher Power* to carry us through and I put my trust in the team of medical experts. Holding on to the hope that Caleb would pull through, it was time to roll up my sleeves and do the gritty stuff needed to save his life.

Breaking my heart, Caleb screamed "No Daddy" continuously for those first few days because it fell on me to pin him down so vital bloods and X-rays could be taken. Pinning down my child, who didn't understand what I was doing to him, to receive painful injections, over and over, tortured me. Never in his little life had he ever had reason to shout: "No Daddy." But being a proper father meant doing anything necessary to protect my child. Thank God for Pedro telling me that night on the bridge that my son needed me. Neither of us could have known just how literal those words would be.

Kirsty's family, and mine, really pulled together during this time. Kirsty and I had gone through a nasty break up but none of that mattered anymore. Life has a way of providing perspective. Had it not been for recovery, I wouldn't have been there. Much like my biological father Billy, I would have been AWOL. Or worse, I could have been dead.

Despite applying my spiritual principles there were still dark moments. I would fall into despair when I analysed things too deeply. For my parents to be back in Edinburgh Sick Kids Hospital as a Nana and Grandad felt cruel. Shayne was back there as an uncle this time. I was back as a father. It all felt so brutal. Seeing my two-year-old son go through the same horrific procedures that my wee brother went through was another injustice I had no control over.

I can't deny there were times I questioned if a loving *Higher Power* truly existed. In a children's cancer ward you see and hear things that torture your soul. One parent stays overnight with their child at a time. Lying on an uncomfortable pull-out bed with what feels like a mosquito net for a blanket, your child sleeps opposite you. Caleb looked so fragile with no hair. Just like his uncle before him. He was attached to machines with wires going in and out of his body. These machines incessantly beep. Nurses come in to take observations every hour (thank God they do, but you don't get to sleep). Some nights I could hear the screams of other children and the weary voices of other parents trying to survive the night. It could truly be a dark, lonely place.

I asked my *Higher Power* why we were back there. Back where DJ had been. At the same time my granny had now become unrecognisable from the woman she had been. I sat in the cancer ward thinking about these things often. Looking at all these innocent babies, I questioned why people like Derek could walk around freely as these innocent children were blighted by such unforgiving illnesses.

Suddenly a simple thought came over me. We live in a human world where illness, accidents and free will exists. Whatever my *Higher Power* is, it doesn't choose for people to suffer. I could point the finger, or I could practice gratitude. Gratitude that we lived in a country which provided life-saving care for my son, where so many others in the world may have died. Gratitude that we lived during times that such treatment was available. Decades earlier it would have been a death sentence. Gratitude that somehow I was clean, in recovery and right by my son's side. I kept faith that unlike my wee brother's battle, this time things would be different.

Recovery taught me not to self-pity and to face life on life's terms. I had to really work hard at acceptance at times. For example, we often ended up back in the very same rooms DJ had been in. Just like DJ, Caleb was painfully poked, prodded and injected. Chemotherapy made his hair fall out, he had a port inserted under his skin and went through operations such as lumbar punctures regularly. Like his uncle before him, Caleb's immune system was compromised. This meant he could become neutropenic which was life-threatening. So he relied on blood transfusions to stay alive whenever he got very poorly. But again, much like his Uncle DJ, Caleb showed great strength, character, determination and spirit. At no point did he ever feel sorry for himself.

All the brutal procedures Caleb had to endure paid off. Diagnosed with *Acute Lymphoblastic Leukaemia* or *ALL*, Caleb's prognosis gave him a 98% chance of recovery. He had the most curable, treatable child cancer. One of the doctors hugged my mum and reassured her, "We're *good* at treating *this* illness, I promise. *This* is not like before with DJ." Such caring humanity sums up all the wonderful staff in the NHS who treated Caleb. Our next aim was for Caleb to reach 'maintenance' when his blood was clear of leukaemia cells, which is like remission. In the meantime we decided it was time to create some good from this horrendous situation, now that things were stabilising. As the saying goes, *out of a crisis comes an opportunity*.

Deciding to focus on positive energy, we made it our mission to use the tool of social media to raise awareness over possible signs of *ALL*. We spoke about what Caleb's signs were. Such as getting ill all the time. Not sleeping. Losing interest in eating and playing. Being lethargic, 'hangy' and crying often. Having a limp, or sore legs. High temperatures. Fevers and sickness. We emphasised limping or sore legs as this was how we caught it. To make sure we didn't put unnecessary fear into people, we reiterated that it was all of these symptoms combined that prompted us to seek urgent medical advice.

I also had an opportunity to make amends with my brother. In honour of DJ *and* Caleb, we carried out two massively successful blood drives in West Lothian. Not only did we raise awareness over the importance of giving blood to save lives—with a massive turnout—I was finally clean enough that I too could give blood. With a lump in my throat, full of emotion, I gave blood and asked DJ to forgive me for not being able to in the past. Which reminds me, if you are able, PLEASE GIVE BLOOD.

We continued our mission to create positive energy as Caleb successfully fought his illness. We raised over £3000 for a local child cancer charity called *Team Jak* with a hair shaving event. It was called *No Hair, Don't Care* which our local newspaper the *West Lothian Courier* covered. My cousin Claire arranged it all. I need to give massive thanks to a gentleman called David Miller (who now runs the Goodfella's Barber Lounge in Easter Bankton, Murieston). David opened his place of business to over forty people on his day off. He shaved everyone's hair and then cleaned it all up, *free of charge*. Throughout the whole process he made everyone feel so welcome. It was such a kind and heartfelt gesture and our family will always be grateful to him.

Suffice to say, hair, beards, legs and chests were shaved and waxed. A local woman who read about the event turned up and had her long, flowing red hair shaved off too. Everyone poignantly clapped. It turned out she too was fighting cancer (sadly she died not long after this). Despite having paid back the money my dad caught me taking from the skydiving fund for DJ, all those years before, I never had a chance to make amends for my actions. This felt like a good start.

In the past I used destructive behaviours to deal with my pain. This time I pulled closer to my recovery. I also went back to my voluntary role supporting people in court as soon as I could. My amends to society and serving others is a life-long commitment. Positivity in the face of adversity was my way of life now.

Having missed months of university, I had fallen behind. But with amazing support from lecturers and friends, work was brought to me in hospital. I studied at Caleb's bedside. Nothing was going to stop me creating a brighter future for my family. To give up my studies would have been conceding that this illness was going to beat us. Nurses would ask how it was possible to study in a ward full of chaos. I simply told them that Caleb's resilience kept me going.

Three months after Caleb's diagnosis we were given the wonderful news we had all been praying for. Doctors couldn't see any more leukaemia cells in his blood. We celebrated in a

143

joyous fashion in a way we never got to for DJ. We knew there was still a journey ahead but thanks to our priceless NHS, my son's life was saved. A few months after that he entered maintenance and could live fully from home again. Though there were still many hospital stays when illnesses needed to be monitored in the ward.

Even in maintenance Caleb still received daily chemotherapy from home (which we gave him). He went for a lumbar puncture every twelve weeks to put chemotherapy into his spinal fluid. He had a host of other medications including steroids (five days a month), which impacted his emotions and moods. They even handed us a bottle of pure morphine to give him whenever his joints got sore (due to the chemo). Just as well I was in recovery now! These times were still hard, but it was a small price to pay for saving his life. We owe that to having an amazing NHS institution.

Whenever Caleb got poorly or had a temperature, we spent a few days in the ward. This is where I really had to apply the tools learned in recovery. Thankfully recovery and family were always there to support us during those difficult times. My mum stayed over often with Caleb if I had to study for exams. What incredible strength that woman showed to put herself back in those wards. She is utterly selfless. We call her 'Supernana'. She was forever putting everyone else first, as always. Everything she does comes from a place of love.

My mum came out with a few crackers as well. During a period in which Caleb was in isolation in his room—to keep him protected—he was on a cycle of steroids. With an operation ahead he was fasting in preparation. Steroid rage ensued as he hungrily and furiously attempted to find food.

144

People had bought him chocolate Easter eggs. So we had to hide them. Upon someone asking my mother what she was hiding, attempting to spell it out she replied, "Caleb's E double eggs." Clearly she meant to say, 'E double G's.' Hilarity ensued once more as we all fell about laughing. As we learned with DJ, sometimes laughter is the best medicine.

The day we got the news of Caleb being in maintenance, Sam and I decided to try for a baby together. A little brother or sister for Caleb. Realising life was too short, we wanted to have a family together. Now I finally knew what true love meant. I remember weeks after we began dating, I took Sam for coffee and confided in her I was a recovering addict. I told her I understood if she wanted to leave. Laughing at my suggestion she replied, "Do I look like I'm going anywhere? And anyway, I kind of figured that much out Aidan." I had lied to her (a white lie) whenever she dropped me at meetings. I used to tell her I was a volunteer who set up chairs.

For Sam to accept me and then stick by my side as my son was diagnosed with cancer, showed she truly loved me for me. And she loved Caleb too. She would never try to be his mother—that was Kirsty's role—but she loved him like a secondary mother figure. Sam taught me I was good enough to be loved. This time I was able to love another human being properly. I am only sorry that past partners experienced that other version of me. But my relationship with Sam was yet another gift in recovery.

Moving in together to a lovely new home more suited to Caleb's immune system, we began trying to get pregnant. I practiced visualising myself graduating university with an Honours Degree. I envisioned my son completely healthy and a baby daughter. I just couldn't get the image of a little sister for Caleb out of my head. These were my first experiences with positive techniques of visualisation and the laws of attraction, highlighting the change in me through recovery. I focused on positive outcomes instead of the inferiority complex I grew up with as an uneducated urbanite.

University life continued to educate me on the self-fulfilling prophecies of young men like me and those I grew up with. Lads who grew up in a 'lad culture' era where violence, substances and 'pulling birds' was all we knew about. Where there were no aspirations to become something great. I thought about all the lads I had troubles with. I didn't think any of them were bad people. We were all part of a generation that didn't really know better, in a new town with a lack of shared history still forming its cultural identity, where access to knowledge or opportunities for education and success were limited. No one ever taught us anything at high school about class inequalities.

My recovery kept growing. I continued to pick up keyrings for clean time and thrived in life as Caleb thrived in his own recovery too. I was really taking an interest in crime now and the reasons why lads like me ended up how I had with addiction. I loved the modules at uni.

Studying DNA evidence in my forensics module, we discussed the re-opened cold case of Angus Sinclair, one of Scotland's most prolific serial killers. At the same time, I was literally involved in supporting family members of his victims during his high court trial. I sat inches away from the killer himself. I'm not saying this to sound up my own arse. It's just that coming down from drugs in the past I would watch crime documentaries and fantasise about the 'pipe-dream' of studying such subjects. That felt like something 'other people' did. Not down and outs like me. But now here I was, studying DNA evidence in university about a trial I was involved in as a support worker.

I ended up supporting people in hundreds of cases at all levels of criminal trial. This included victims of sexual abuse. Historical sexual abuse as well. What happened with Derek had been firmly compartmentalised in my mind. But through my education in social sciences and witnessing first-hand what a victim (known in Scottish courts as a 'complainer') went through, I felt I might never report what happened.

Jimmy Saville and Rolf Harris both being exposed as sexual predators forced me to re-live my experiences. And the *#MeToo* movement too. Despite that movement being a force for good, it felt to me like a feminist view of men as antagonists. It was a very gender specific discussion. Male (perpetrator) vs female (victim). I had no idea where I fit into it. It only confused me even more.

Seeing my son fight cancer like DJ had made me think about how young and vulnerable I was when I began talking to Derek online. When I think of DJ passing away at fourteen—despite how wise he had become ahead of his years—he was just a boy in the grand scheme of things. I too was just a boy when Derek and I began speaking. I was barely fourteen. At our first meeting when I was fifteen, I was still a boy. Young, naive and vulnerable. Continuing to have him in my life after turning sixteen really fucked my head up. Legal consent in the UK. Sixteen. In America I'd still have been viewed legally as a minor. But not in the UK. So I kept blaming myself. Even with all I was learning.

I also had conflicting feelings about the criminal justice system in Scotland. In Scotland we rely on corroboration, meaning two independent pieces of evidence are required beyond reasonable doubt to gain a conviction. On the one hand this protects innocent people from being unjustly locked up for accusations that lack evidence beyond a person's own testimony. It would be detrimental for someone to be found guilty so easily on a false accusation. Yet, corroboration was also detrimental for people like me. I supported people through some very unforgiving processes at court in which the corroboration law meant their cases fell apart.

I knew that providing a statement to the police meant from that moment onward I had no control. If the police deemed there was enough evidence, it would be passed on to the procurator fiscal who would decide if there was enough evidence to go to trial. I worried about revisiting all that pain. Especially if it didn't make it to trial. If it did go to trial, I couldn't back out or retract my statement if I changed my mind. I couldn't even hire a lawyer of my own choosing. In Scotland a procurator fiscal or *advocate depute*, acts on behalf of the Crown and society. In my experience this can feel extremely impersonal. I had witnessed many victims (complainers) turning up on the day of their trial with no idea of what to expect. And many had no idea who was supposed to be acting on their behalf.

Upon being called to give evidence the 'complainer' is then interrogated or *cross examined* by a defence lawyer, who will find any means necessary to pick holes in their evidence.

Again I felt conflicted here. On the one hand, I felt that if I were accused of a crime I would want a hardened defence lawyer on my side. However, I viewed many victims who took the stand and had to justify themselves to a stranger. A lawyer who would jump on any mistakes they made with what their fractured memory could recall. They used legal terminology that the victim wasn't familiar with, in a setting the victim had no experience in. At times the system victimised people again (secondary victimisation). Which to me was another harsh injustice. And in Scotland there are three possible outcomes: guilty, not guilty or not proven. A not proven verdict means there is no closure for anyone involved. So, to be honest, the idea of it all fucking terrified me.

When I thought back to meeting Derek, my memory was fractured in places. Diminished by years of trying to avoid the trauma through active addiction. My biggest worry was if anyone would believe me. I didn't want to be treated differently either. I didn't know any other men my age who had been a victim of this. I felt so lost. So confused. I didn't know what to do. I kept blaming myself.

I *still* believed meeting Derek was my own fault and my own choosing. Even as I supported my son fighting cancer. Worked my way through recovery. Volunteered in criminal trials. Worked in homeless hostels. Studied for a degree. I believed that continuing a relationship with him in any form after turning sixteen, meant I clearly wanted to meet him. My mind would go back and forth between convincing myself I had been groomed, to thinking that having contact with him after sixteen meant it was my free choice. It was fucking relentless.

But then an opportunity came my way. My university offered free counselling sessions to discuss my son's illness. During these sessions I found myself talking to my counsellor about my addiction and recovery. Whilst discussing the sexual part of my addiction—and all the shame I felt—I blurted out Derek's name. I started to talk about all those years ago when I had met him. The counsellor astounded me with his take on things.

He told me that I didn't stop being a child the moment I turned sixteen. He said the damage had already been done. The grooming had already happened. He told me it wasn't my fault. We acknowledged that Grandad should have hidden his porn collection better. That I sought out porn as a habit. That I engaged in conversations with this older man when I was a young teenager. We acknowledged me feeling abandoned by my biological father Billy. That I had a tough relationship with my dad. But my counsellor told me that none of that was to blame for what Derek had done to me. No one else, not even me when I continued to be involved with him after I had turned sixteen, was to blame for what happened, other than Derek. Through intensive counselling, I was finally able to see that I had been a vulnerable child taken advantage of by a predator.

With all this information on a continuous loop in my head, I kept moving forward with my life. Something I have learned by looking back—just like when Steve Jobs discussed joining the dots up—is that my *Higher Power* has always been in my life guiding me. Even years before I heard of recovery. This isn't just a belief system. I know it in my heart. Arriving home early from university one morning, I found my partner

150

on the couch. She had come home ill from work and was watching the TV show *This Morning* with Phillip Schofield and Holly Willoughby. Neither of us were meant to be home that morning, so I guess you could say I wasn't *supposed* to catch the show, which we never watched anyway.

As I sat down at my computer desk something made my ears twitch. I overheard Phillip and Holly talking about the topic of grooming and the behaviour of predators. My heart began dancing around as if I was back on eccies. Something came over me. I tried something I had never attempted before. I googled Derek's name and some of the areas he claimed to work in. What I discovered disturbed me in ways I struggled to comprehend.

Chapter Twelve:
Never Quite Done

I often imagine what I would do if I could travel back in time to intercept the fifteen-year-old boy who stood there, lost, waiting on Derek. I wish I could grab him and hug him. I would tell him he was worth so much more than this. I would tell him he was loved and still had so much to learn about why things felt as they did. I'd take his hand and lead him home to safety. But I cannot go back. Just like I can't save my brother from dying the way I always wished I could. Just like I had no control over Caleb getting diagnosed. Just like I can't undo the pain I caused other people.

Sometimes, whilst wasted, I used to fantasise that my grandad would show up, as if he had driven down from heaven. In my fantasy he would swing open the passenger door in his taxi, smile at me—whilst wearing that signature bunnet of his—and say to me, "C'mon son, let's get out of here," then take me with him. But now I realise that was never meant to happen. My purpose was to face this one day. That day had arrived.

Opening on my screen before me was a solitary picture of Derek. Alongside his image, which felt sickening to look at, was a testimony depicting a very different persona to the man

I had met. Derek described himself as a loving Christian man. He praised God and told others to hand their lives over to Jesus. He had been in ministry as a pastor. He had been a religious youth worker. It went on and on. All about his family. The way he served the community. He was a saint by the words in his testimony.

He spoke about the loss of his son. But the dates didn't match up. It became clear to me that his son had been very ill when he met me. He had used the impending death of his own son to manipulate me. Having a child fighting a serious illness myself, and after losing DJ, this was another heinous reality to discover.

I just stared at this religious testimony in shock and disbelief. It was hard to take in. Gushing over his family life and his love for other people, he even described how he would tour the country as a pastor warning people of various dangers in society. Guiding people to live a more Christian-like lifestyle. If it wasn't so fucking tragic, I would have laughed at the disgusting hypocrisy. I am certain he didn't warn people of the true dangers in this world, such as predators hiding in the guise of religious preachers, who groom vulnerable young boys.

Once the shock had dissipated, I felt a fury ignite within me. A fucking rage I had never allowed myself to feel before. For the first time in my life I realised I was a victim. I realised fully in that moment that I had been groomed and abused. Realising his status in society compared with the vulnerable suicidal teenager I had been, finally allowed me to see things clearly. The feeling was so fresh and tender that it was impossible to stop it spilling out in front of Sam. I had never told her before. I had barely mentioned this to a soul for all the years I carried it around. Blaming myself.

It must have felt nonsensical to Sam when I erupted. Like a burning lava shooting up my body and flying out my mouth in a verbal tirade. I was unable to hide my anger as I told her about my experiences with Derek. Sam stayed calm. She listened and understood as she always did. Patient and empathetic—qualities that make her such a great nurse—she loved me through the moment. It was ground-breaking news for her and yet she never made it about her. Not once. My mother and brother Shayne had a vague idea that something had happened in my past, but I knew the whole truth was about to come tumbling out of me.

Being in recovery, I knew the next thing I had to do was go and speak to my sponsor for guidance. I was torn. Not only was I groomed and taken advantage of by an older man, but this had been a so-called religious man. A man who spent over a year grooming a vulnerable fourteen-year-old boy before finally taking him to a hotel. Part of me wanted to move on and keep what control I had left, but it ate away at me like maggots on a flesh wound. I worried about his role as a 'youth worker'. I couldn't stop thinking about other potential victims. It kept me up at night.

Guided by prayer and my sponsor, I decided that with Caleb still fighting cancer and me still in early recovery, it wasn't the right time to act on it. Throwing myself into the sometimes-brutal criminal justice system was a terrifying thought. Especially about an experience I was still trying to understand. Unlike many other victims I had plenty of experience in criminal trials. I had studied many relevant

154

theories too. That was another reason I talked myself in-and-out of going to the police for so long. Carrying on with my life I continued to excel in recovery, proud to be clean as I watched my baby boy grow through his recovery as well.

Coming to terms with the magnitude of it all weighed heavily on me. Over and over I thought of other victims. Especially as I still supported people at court. *Higher Power* moments were still reminding me I was on the right path. One day, as I was in the witness room supporting someone, a familiar looking police witness caught my attention. It was Pedro, the policeman who saved me from the bridge. He saw me too. Without exposing me, he simply smiled and nodded. Just like his conduct on the bridge, he was a class act and I am grateful to him for my life. It was a beautiful moment.

I kept moving forward with life, but knew I had to report what happened with Derek. I agonised about it constantly. I knew the day was coming. But not yet. I continued practising visualisation. With recovery guiding me, my positive images came true. I graduated university with a 2:1 Honours Degree in Social Sciences: with Criminology and Sociology. My son was healthy and well and my baby daughter Leah had already been born, to my now fiancée Sam. We gave Leah the middle name Margaret, after my beloved granny. Rather than stealing my mother's peace of mind, as I did in my active addiction, she stood by my side proudly watching me achieve great heights.

Graduation day 2017 was a special moment. One of the speakers told us we were ready to go out into the world and use our newfound knowledge, experience and qualifications to make a difference in society. After everything I had been through that statement was more like a moral code than a positive affirmation. I took on a job that I loved, working with people who lived with a blood borne virus such as HIV or hepatitis C. Considering my background as an addict, it was a special role with a fantastic organisation. Important work.

As my contract came to an end in that role, I had everything I could have wished for. I was two-and-a-half years clean. I had my degree. I had completed my 12-step programme. I was sponsoring someone and taking them through the 12 steps too. I had my two children and a beautiful fiancée who I loved and that loved me back. We lived in a gorgeous wee home and had no financial worries. Caleb was responding well to his treatment. And then the unthinkable happened. I relapsed.

The relapse was extremely brief, but it snapped my mental health in two like a piece of liquorice. The truth is I had become arrogant, complacent and cocky about my recovery. I rarely went to meetings or tried to connect with others in recovery anymore. I tried to do it alone. Completing the 12 steps, getting my degree, making good money and seeing myself as a 'professional' went to my head. My ego took off. It was a harsh lesson to learn. Life humbled me quickly. Very soon the suicidal thoughts came back. It was hard to imagine myself back there again.

Yet again someone was on hand to save my life. A fellow addict in recovery called Dave. I sent him a WhatsApp message. I told him I felt I had no choice but to end my life. Dave reminded me how important I had been to his recovery. He told me to "get back to a meeting." It was purely that simple advice of 'keep coming back'. So I listened to him. I went back to a meeting.

As I staggered back in, broken, beaten and with a bruised ego, I was met with warm hugs and welcomed home. I am forever grateful to Dave and the two lads in the meeting, Eddie and Boydy, who made me feel taken care of in a moment where I was so fragile. They didn't judge me for falling from the pedestal I had put myself on. I have never taken my recovery for granted since that moment and I never will again.

After throwing myself back into recovery, I took a job as a criminal justice support worker. I worked with hidden victims of abuse such as males and people who were LGBT. It was in this job that my boss introduced me to a book called *Chancers* by Susan Stelling and Graham MacIndoe. It was based largely on Graham's addiction and recovery. A Scottish man (from West Lothian too), which drew me to the story. And then I realised that the year before I had seen his photo gallery in Edinburgh. As a photographer he captured his addiction so poignantly. It had stuck with me. Reading his story planted a seed. I also went back to volunteering in criminal trials and applied for a master's degree in social work. I even got myself a driver's license finally after one of my mum's old friends kindly bought me a block of lessons.

I got myself a new sponsor too. A big, cheery, burly lad my age who I had known for over ten years. His name was Scott and he looked like a cross between Richard Branson and Thor. The first thing I told him about was the burden of Derek. I didn't blame that, or my son's ongoing battle with cancer, for my relapse. In recovery you need to be accountable for your own choices. It was my choice to relapse. But I knew this trauma was unresolved and without closure it remained a risk to my mental health.

Whilst doing step-work with my sponsor, he offered his opinion. Scott felt that rather than a sex addict, I was a degradation addict. His insight astounded me and echoed what that considerate dominatrix in Vancouver had suggested. This terminology felt much more authentic than being addicted to sex. Having physical sex had almost nothing to do with my behaviours. The very fact that the word sex was involved made it feel taboo for so many years. Like some stigmatised shame I had to hide from everyone. Telling people I abused substances felt like a breeze in comparison. You don't want people to think you are forever hooked on sex and porn, or for them to associate the words 'sex addict' with anything sick or illegal. But most of all, it made me feel exposed, embarrassed and was cringey to talk about.

Recovery was the foundation for my life again but both Scott and I knew that I needed to seek 'outside help'. Meaning therapy. It was clear I needed the guidance of a professional. The end goal was to report what happened to the police. To stop Derek from hurting anyone else. I was finally ready. But before I could do that, life was on life's terms once more. Granny passed away.

For seventeen years my family watched Granny struggle with horrendous illnesses. So much that she was never fully able to understand the illnesses DJ and Caleb suffered. My mother strenuously tried to care for Granny at home, but she needed specialist support. Granny spent her final years in a nursing home. We loved her every step of the way. All the way through those excruciatingly hard times. In her final four days, we camped out at her bedside living on tea, coffee and takeaways, much like in the cancer wards with DJ and Caleb. We sang Irish songs to her such as 'Wild Rover' as she slipped away, taking her final breaths. Finally, Granny found peace and was reunited with Grandad.

Upon receiving her ashes, we went to the same spot where we had released Grandad's ashes seventeen years prior, as a family. Neil, my eldest cousin, who Grandad once named his taxi company after (Neil's Cabs), was wearing Grandad's signature bunnet. We all knew that bunnet belonged with Neil. It fills my heart with joy knowing he has it. True to Granny's humorous nature, we gathered in a circle, each with a handful of ashes, and threw them into the windy autumn air shouting, "Foook off!!" in our best Irish accents.

Standing there, clean and in the moment once more, I watched my precious family love each other. Caleb ran around shouting after my mother, "Nana, I have got Gee-Gee on my trousers!" with Gee-Gee being our name for great granny. She left a legacy behind. In fact, it was after she passed away that I became overwhelmed by this... feeling. It was a furious urge, like a starving dream waiting to be fed with belief. It was as if Granny was saying, "Write a book. Write a book. Write a book." So I went home and sat down at my computer desk. I began typing. There was only once place to begin. The thought struck me with dread. But I did it anyway. Chapter one. Groomed.

As I was writing chapter two of this book, weeks after Granny dying, I then found out that my biological father Billy had passed away from cancer. I had reached out to him multiple times since he was diagnosed two years earlier and attempted a reconciliation. He was never interested. He died without me ever getting to meet him in person. I was denied what should have been a birth right—meeting my biological father. No one invited us to the funeral either. I would never get the closure I was seeking from him. I understood that he had suffered his own traumas in life. This much I had been told. I knew he was an addict like me. So I tried to have empathy. But I still struggled with never getting to know who he was. Never getting to look him in the eye.

I guess I will never know the man. I will never get to piece together those final parts of the jigsaw of my identity for that half of my biological family. I am blessed, however, to have two families in my life now—my 'belly button family' and my 'recovery family'. I am truly loved.

I remained focused on recovery and on my family to cope with those big losses. I moved on to another job as an advocacy worker for people with addictions and mental health issues. The role involved tackling a wide range of factors in West Lothian—the county I live in which hosts the town of Livingston—with the sole purpose of improving things for addicts in my area. I also gained a place on that master's degree course for social work, with a desire to do more specialist work with addiction, mental health and offending behaviour. Things were thriving again, and it was now time to seek out therapy.

Nerves were on me for the first session. We met at an old church in Linlithgow. It felt ironic meeting in a church. It wasn't far from Livingston. The therapist was a younger guy. He had a quirky yet trendy style, with trainers that reminded

160

me of a hipster. His glasses suited him, and the empathy oozed out from his voice. I felt safe. We discussed what I wanted to gain from our sessions. That part was clear as day. I needed to report Derek to the police. I opened my soul like a portal to the past. Things came out that I never thought I would tell another man. After the session was over, he 'checked in' with me to make sure I still felt safe. I told him I did. We arranged another appointment for a fortnight later to give me time to process things.

When I arrived home, I spoke to Sam and told her all about the session. As she folded up clothes in our bedroom I sat on the edge of the bed. The fear was back. I was talking myself out of it. She put down the clothes and gently sat down next to me. With her beautiful blue eyes looking into mine she asked a simple question, "What's holding you back babe?"

"I just need to wait for the right time. I don't know when the right time is. There is so much going on in life. There has just never been a good time," I explained.

Sam listened intently to my wobble. Once I stopped ranting, she opened her mouth to speak. Again she floored me with a truth articulated so simply. "Babe, there is never going to be a right time. There will always be a reason not to do it until the day you do it." With that she went back to folding the clothes.

Something must have happened in my sleep that night. The next day I did something I never imagined I would ever do. I picked up the phone and dialled 101 for the police. I asked if they had a specialist department to report historical sexual abuse. The woman on the line told me it was them I had to report it to. So, there it was, the scariest moment of my life, almost two decades in the making, and I was to explain it all down the phone to a stranger. For once in my life that 'fuck it' mentality paid off. Because I said to myself, "Fuck it, this is getting done," and I told her everything. She then arranged for me to see two police officers at the station a few days later.

It was early doors, but I felt elated to have finally done it. I knew the scary part was still to come. I phoned Scott, my mum and Sam. They were all shocked that I had just gone for it. But they were ecstatic for me too. With the police appointment getting closer, I couldn't help myself. I started to look for him online. I was ready to face him. But what I discovered was like a punch in the gut.

Having figured out his full name and where he lived, I searched him thoroughly. I was certain what I had found was true. He was dead. There was no picture anywhere, other than the testimony. But he was dead and had been for a good few years. The eulogy had his full name and where he was from. All that time I wanted to avoid a criminal trial and now I would never get a chance to look him in the eye. Years wasted worrying that no one would believe me, and he was already gone. It felt cruel. But then something occurred to me. There may be other victims. His status in society meant that he could have known other abusers too. I still had to report it.

Sitting in front of two young male police officers to finally tell my story was a strange experience. The room felt cold and clinical, but their conduct was slow and relaxed. Full of compassion. One was about my age and the other must have been barely twenty. The older officer was the experienced one and he explained that the young cop would lead the questions under his supervision to gain experience.

Surprisingly I felt OK about it. But it was bizarre to bare my soul to this young man with the face of a teenager. They both looked shellshocked as they listened, with intervals of tears from me as I recalled the sordid things that happened.

Ultimately, they explained that this was unlike anything they had dealt with before. They were just normal cops and would be back dealing with domestics in the street soon. But the older cop looked at me and said the most important thing, "We can't prove anything at this stage, but we believe you. We believe all of that happened to you. We believe you were groomed." With those words, he gave me permission to unclip the burden from my shoulders and drop it to the floor like a heavy sack of bricks.

Many things had worried me for so long that shouldn't have. When I spoke to Derek for the last time on MSN and he said to me "I didn't meet you until you were sixteen" it really messed up my head. For years I believed we must have met when I was legally old enough to consent. Therefore it was my choice and I was to blame. The police explained that the age of sixteen was a grey area and they would have investigated the grooming process that began when I was fourteen.

I also worried about my memory. I could remember major things but so many details were gone or jumbled up in my head. An example was when they asked me if Derek had penetrated me. It felt as clinical as the room I was in, but it was an important question. I remembered quite easily some of the things he had done to me. The use of his fingers and tongue which makes me feel violated to still have in my memories. I could never forget his penis in between my bum cheeks. But I genuinely could never remember how far into

163

me he went. It was another thing that had stopped me getting help for so long. That one fractured memory. I had seen people on the witness stand crucified in historical sexual abuse trials based on flimsy memory.

But I was to learn again that it wasn't a weakness. The police seemed extremely understanding about my fractured memory. They believed me and they had enough from my statement to send this to a detective to investigate. They told me I was courageous. They praised my career choices and my wish to use my pain to help others. They treated me with dignity. They made me feel human after describing the must inhumane experiences.

A detective did interview me again and it was done at my pace. I wasn't made to relive everything, but I did have to go back over some parts. Her investigation concluded by discovering the dreaded truth that I already knew. He had died just less than a decade ago. She told me she wished she could have investigated this all the way for me. A consolation prize was that he died alone. But he wasn't known to police. That was another blow to the ribs. I know there are other victims of his out there. I feel it in my gut. In fact he told me about a 'boy' he would meet in London. That memory just came back to me as I re-read this chapter. Only strengthening my belief that memories can be locked away.

What does feel reassuring is knowing that if anyone else comes forward now my evidence will corroborate theirs. It has crossed my mind as well about the laptop Derek would bring when we met. It makes me wonder what was on it. Was I on it? I wonder if he had links to other abusers. I may never know. But if there *are* any other abusers linked to Derek who are discovered, my evidence is sitting in a file waiting to be used. Most importantly though, finally I was free. At the time of writing this I have just started therapy with another psychologist to work on the aftermath of the abuse. The behaviours. The self-harming aspect of my sexuality. It has already been an awakening.

There is absolutely nothing wrong with taking part in a fetish or having a kink. I still enjoy many of those. It is the patterns of abuse-seeking that I am working on. I am already learning that it is common in male victims to seek out this kind of abuse. That it has been my way of 'controlling' how I am abused. Also, that it is common for victims to sabotage relationships and hurt others before they can be hurt. I learned too that there is a process of 'setting up', meaning to seek out abuse and either see it through or bail on it before it happens. Which is what lead to many patterns of behaviours that left me in turmoil and confused. The therapy is ongoing.

My hope is that this book can reach others too. Whether someone has suffered from abuse, mental health issues or any form of addiction. I want people to know that the gift of recovery does exist. It is important to say too, that you do not have to be a victim of abuse to be an addict of any kind. I would also recommend reading Russel Brand's amazing breakdown of addiction and recovery in his book *Freedom from Our Addictions*. Listening to the audiobook gave me the courage to face my sexual addiction without shame. Thank you, Russel.

I want men to know that it is safe to speak out. Of course I want everyone to feel that way. But as a man I have always felt like it wasn't safe to talk about these things. Speaking out has saved me. Speaking out has led me to write about it too. I see so many other men out there suffering. We need to unlearn the street rules we grew up with about tearing each other down. We need to elevate each other. Support each other. Champion one another. We must end the stigma, stereotypes and shame. I owe my ability to speak openly and honestly to my recovery.

One day at a time, I am clean and living life to the fullest. My *Higher Power* has given me a life beyond my wildest dreams. I have gone from being a hopeless using addict living on a mattress to being surrounded by a loving family and life-long friends. I have gone from being uneducated to having an honours degree. In fact, at the time of writing this I am successfully at the halfway point of my master's degree in social work. I will graduate not long after this book is released.

No longer am I having one-man parties or acting like a cardboard gangster. Neither am I getting all dressed up with nowhere to go but my living room in a paranoid psychosis, with the blinds closed and a table full of cocaine and vodka. Fear doesn't consume me anymore. Instead of being emotionally shutdown, crippled by feelings of worthlessness and despair, I am thriving, developing and growing. I have learned how to love and be loved, how to help and be helped. I am just a guy who found recovery and was shown the way out of addiction. For me it will always be a life-long programme of maintenance.

I could not have done any of this on my own. I credit my *Higher Power* for saving me and my recovery network with keeping me well. I also must credit my family for never giving up on me. To Sam and my kids for loving me in ways I never knew possible. And to my mum. The strongest human being I have ever known in my life. Someone who believed in me and loved me unconditionally, even when I was in the gutter. Someone who never gave up on me. I love you mum with all my heart. We both know that 'DJ' is always guiding us.

Since I wrote this book Caleb has successfully completed treatment and has been cancer free for over a year. We were blessed with an amazing free holiday to Florida after he finished treatment. Given to us by a charity called *Rays of Sunshine*, it showed how far Kirsty and I had come as the holiday was for me, Kirsty and Caleb (we all went together). As usual Sam was nothing but supportive. This was all about Caleb. We stayed in a place called *Give Kids The World Village* which was like living in a magical fairyland for the week. All expenses were paid. The sun shone all week and we went to every Disney theme park. We had a fast pass, meaning we got to go straight on to every ride and skip all the queues. Caleb's dream had been to swim with dolphins and *Rays of Sunshine* made this come true, arranging it through a place called *Discovery Cove*.

I also found out that Alan passed away. He had cancer too. That big fucking C word that I have encountered so many times. I had the chance to let him know just how important he was to my life. Meeting him changed the course of everything. We crossed paths for only a short time, but the impact was life-changing. It appears that my *Higher Power* has consistently put people on my path to save my life. That's not delusions of grandeur or anything. It is just impossible for me to deny. Some may call those things coincidences. I am not that naïve anymore as to believe in a concept like coincidence.

Now I have dreams of becoming an author. To connect with other people on a grander scale. Mum tells me I always wanted to be a writer. But I traded in my dreams for addiction. Well now I have traded them back! Recovery taught me how to survive but it also taught me to take positive risks. We only get one shot at this life, so living in fear is futile. I have already started work on another book. A Scottish working-class fiction based loosely on some of the people I grew up with. A mystery based on the trance/drug culture set in the early 2000s in West Lothian. I aim to pitch that to publishers by 2021.

The title of this chapter has two meanings. I could never control addiction on my own. In my addiction I always had to keep feeding that insatiable craving for more. I never found fulfilment. Hence the saying: 'One is too many and a thousand never enough.' A using addict, whether sex, substances or something else, is never quite done. But now I don't think of it that way. Despite all the depraved, desperate rock bottoms, it was over the moment I asked for help. When I finally surrendered. That is when I began to heal. Even when I thought I was all alone, I am here as living proof to tell you, I wasn't! Now I know that even when you think there is no hope left and it is all over for you, so long as there is oxygen in your lungs, you are NEVER QUITE DONE.

I will finish on this. One of my biggest fears about speaking out was in case this got back to Derek's family. I don't want to hurt them or tarnish anyone's memory of their loved one. My brother Shayne removed this concern from me by stating, "That's not your burden to carry, Aidan. Fuck him." Sometimes you just need your big brother to give it to you straight. Now my truth is set free. Now this burden is gone.

My name is Aidan and I am an addict. I am grateful to be clean, thank you.

About the Author

Born in Ladywell, Livingston, Aidan Martin is a debuting memoirist. His first book, *Euphoric Recall*, discusses in detail his recovery from addiction and many traumas including sexual abuse. Aidan is a fiancé to his beautiful partner and a proud father of two beautiful children. He currently works as a mental health and addictions worker as well as studying social work at master's degree level. In 2017 he gained an Honours Degree in Social Sciences: with Criminology and Sociology. As a grateful recovering addict, Aidan is heavily involved in the recovery scene. He is currently working on a Scottish working-class fiction around trance culture.

For more info visit: www.aidanmartinauthor.co.uk and www.facebook.com/aidanmartinauthor

About the Illustrator

Mark Deans is an artist and musician based in Livingston, Scotland. He is the creator of the cover art, an ink drawing on paper created specifically for this book.

Mark met Aidan in Livingston as a child, outside from sun up to sun down and grew into manhood alongside him. Mark took up painting and art as a second creative outlet alongside music. His pursuit started as a coping mechanism and although self-taught, Mark has garnered several commissions and a recent online exhibition.

For more info visit: www.facebook.com/MarkDeansMusic/ and www.instagram.com/darkmeansart/

About Guts Publishing

Established in May 2019, we are an independent publisher in London. The name came from the obvious—it takes guts to publish just about anything. We are the home to the freaks and misfits of the literary world.

We like uncomfortable topics. Our tagline: Ballsy books about life. Our thinking: the book market has enough ball-less books and we're happy to shake things up a bit.

Euphoric Recall is our debut memoir. We are delighted to bring this story to you, and hope you've enjoyed reading it. Well done, Aidan Martin.

Cyber Smut (Sept 2020), our second anthology, is a collection of fiction, nonfiction and poetry about how the internet and technology impact our lives, our sexuality and how we love.

Stories About Penises (Nov 2019), our debut anthology, is a collection of fiction, nonfiction and poetry about, well, exactly what it sounds like. To quote a prominent Australian author, 'Quite possibly the best title of the year.' We think so too.

Our website: gutspublishing.com.
Our email: gutspublishing@gmail.com

Thank you for reading, and thank you for your support!